Everyday Thoughts

Everyday Thoughts

A Collection of Devotional Readings
for Thinking Christians

Phillip Michael Garner

WIPF & STOCK · Eugene, Oregon

EVERYDAY THOUGHTS
A Collection of Devotional Readings for Thinking Christians

Copyright © 2017 Phillip Michael Garner. All rights reserved. Except for brief quotations in critical publications or reviews, no part of this book may be reproduced in any manner without prior written permission from the publisher. Write: Permissions, Wipf and Stock Publishers, 199 W. 8th Ave., Suite 3, Eugene, OR 97401.

Wipf & Stock
An Imprint of Wipf and Stock Publishers
199 W. 8th Ave., Suite 3
Eugene, OR 97401

www.wipfandstock.com

PAPERBACK ISBN: 978-1-5326-1828-4
HARDCOVER ISBN: 978-1-4982-4372-8
EBOOK ISBN: 978-1-4982-4371-1

Manufactured in the U.S.A.   SEPTEMBER 1, 2017

Contents

Preface | *vii*

Reading One: When God was a Child | 1

Reading Two: The Childlike Qualities of Jesus People | 5

Reading Three: Not a Book for Children | 8

Reading Four: Language Must Always be in Color | 12

Reading Five: Myth and Romanticism | 15

Reading Six: Absolute Love Demonstrated in Human Beings | 20

Reading Seven: Christianity the Cure for Human Hubris | 25

Reading Eight: Called to Renounce Violence | 28

Reading Nine: Faith and Doubt | 32

Reading Ten: Reflections on the Disposition of Sorrow and Joy | 35

Reading Eleven: Flesh from the Earth and Glory from Above | 39

Reading Twelve: Promises in Contrast | 43

Reading Thirteen: Meaning and Suffering | 49

Reading Fourteen: The Apocalypse: A Genre for Human Madness | 56

Reading Fifteen: Redemption: The End of History | 61

Reading Sixteen: A Psychology of Illness in Psalm 38 | 64

Reading Seventeen: The Struggles of Reading and Writing Theology | 68

Reading Eighteen: Theological Musings | 70

Reading Nineteen: God's Word, Archaic Laws, and Torah as Teaching | 75

CONTENTS

Reading Twenty: Spiritual Intelligence | 84

Reading Twenty-One: Responsible Faith | 88

Reading Twenty-Two: Adam's Lament | 92

Reading Twenty-Three: Jesus and the Roman Tax | 96

Reading Twenty-Four: Ending Poverty by Becoming Human | 99

Reading Twenty-Five: The American Oligarchy | 101

Reading Twenty-Six: Josiah's Failed Reforms and the Book of Jonah | 105

Reading Twenty-Seven: A Missional Reading of Luke's Pentecost Narrative | 108

Reading Twenty-Eight: God's Imagination | 112

Reading Twenty-Nine: The Crucified God-Man | 115

Reading Thirty: An Intertextual Theology from Genesis and Job on the Human Condition | 121

Reading Thirty-One: Don't Blame the Serpent | 128

Reading Thirty-Two: Sexuality, Temporality, and Gender | 132

Reading Thirty-Three: Jacob's Dream | 136

Reading Thirty-Four: Land, Peace, and Promises from God | 140

Reading Thirty-Five: A Cognitive Field of Hermeneutics | 148

Reading Thirty-Six: The Teacher and Christian Education | 153

Reading Thirty-Seven: God of Freedom not of Control | 156

Reading Thirty-Eight: Sensitivity to Evil | 161

Reading Thirty-Nine: God in the Court of Human Experience | 164

Reading Forty: Reading the Lazarus Stories | 168

Preface

Everyday Thoughts is a collection of daily readings for thinking Christians. The following pages offer forty biblical and theological essays for spiritual and intellectual upbuilding. Loving God includes the intellectual effort of thinking deeply about God, creation, and reality. Loving God through contemplation rooted in faith and thought, built upon scripture, is a spiritual discipline.

This book is written to offer a devotional for believers who enjoy concise pieces on biblical and theological subjects. Each essay is preceded by a poem and contains text box quotes for contemplation. The essays are written to encourage deep thinking. It is my hope that the reader discovers inspirational ideas and thoughts that challenge, enlighten, and stimulate contemplative spirituality with insight into God, humanity, and creation.

All forty essays are written for persons familiar with the biblical text and theology. However, I have attempted to make each piece accessible to any thinking adult. I personally enjoy stimulating ideas and find my day is fuller when my mind and heart are continually running a background program wrestling with ideas.

These essays are a product of my engagement with a learning community of believers. Each essay reflects my efforts to offer them thoughts and ideas in response to their missional and intellectual practice. I share these works of love and thought in hope that they will inspire and bless the reader.

Reading One

When God was a Child

Up from the Ground

I'm human to the core
Up from the ground
My weaknesses make me feel
I have repented
I have embraced my sin and owned it
God still loves me
Like a Child
I have soared to great heights
I have fallen
Looking up I hear him call
Turning to see him at my side
I know him
He is my friend
I walk alone
I walk with him
I'm not double-minded
I am tested
Love never gives up
Love wins
Rest comes
The struggle continues
I live in two worlds
I am a Christian

When God was a Child

The birth of Jesus speaks to the wonder of what it means to be human. That the infant was, in essence, God wrapped in all the trappings of flesh directs all of us to look upon human beginnings with awe and reverence for our creator. Even our children can be filled with the Spirit. What is this but good news? God has joined the creation, and now, when speaking of God, we must include that part of what it means to be God is to be human. How could human life be decreed with any greater proclamation of sacredness than this singular truth? If we believe this to be so, then we must open our arms, like our Lord, to all of humanity in all her wondrous differences and variations of color, culture, and self-expression.

> God has joined the creation and now when speaking of God we must include that part of what it means to be God is to be human.

Like us, God in humanness, experienced being and becoming human. During the course of his sojourn on earth, Jesus would grow to embrace a matured realization of self; but along the way, the *logos* played and looked at the world with the eyes of a child. This experience for God is observable for us in the open innocence of children who believe simply because they are alive. However, east of Eden, innocence cannot be kept, consciousness and maturity insist otherwise. Jesus, like all children, felt the loss of innocence (not through personal sin but by observance), for his sensitivity to evil was attuned to the onslaught of sin in the world. Jesus kept his sensitivity to evil and preserved a matured innocence.

> [40] *The child grew and became strong, filled with wisdom; and the favor of God was upon him.*
>
> LUKE 2:40

Jesus sees in children an admirable innocence, an innocence that is essential for entering and experiencing the reign of God. Jesus eschews the adult world of competitiveness for positions of power over others. He uses children to call us to return to the innocence of wonder and awe when viewing the creation. He beckons us to trust God with what appears as an absurd naivety, which he himself maintained in the face of evil. You might wish to protest and declare that such manner of living will end in death; it is impractical. I agree that the demands of Jesus are impractical; the same can be said of all our systems of control that govern our lives. The impractical demands of Jesus lead to life and peace, while most people live with and do not challenge the systems of the world that only reproduce the cycles of violence that permeate human history.

Jesus overtly points, with explicit clarity, to the power of children as instructive for removing adult illusions of expediency. It seems that Jesus thinks we adults take ourselves too seriously and fail to enter the reign of God where childlike joy—even laughter over simplicity—is not impeded by the vanity of desire. Jesus will take a small child in his arms, possibly an infant or a toddler, and claim that to receive this one is to receive him. We are invited to act like Jesus did in relation to children: with patience, love, and acceptance—with an awareness of their inherent possibility to be guides for manifesting the social dynamics necessary for entering the kingdom of God.

> *36 Then he took a little child and put it among them; and taking it in his arms, he said to them, 37 "Whoever welcomes one such child in my name welcomes me, and whoever welcomes me welcomes not me but the one who sent me."*
>
> MARK 9:36–37

It is evident that God cares deeply about the inclusion of children into the social fabric of daily living. Keeping children close to daily activity brings innocence into an adult world of exclusion, a world that needs the contribution of their innocence. We have recognized the need of children for adults and not recognized the need of adults for children. Jesus, the last Adam, began life as a child. In effect, God has a childhood; he possesses the memories of being a child. God entered the creation as a human being, and so all the wonder of being a developing human—of being a little kid—belongs to God's joy and experience.

By separating ourselves into age and gender groups, we lose our humanity. Like history lost, childhood is forgotten, and old age is an apocalypse to be avoided. The desperation for community in our postmodern youth movements and churches is an experiment certain to fail if all humanity—children, youth, and the aged—are not embraced. An intellectual needs the imagination of a child to search the existential realities that reveal God; a child needs to learn the power of a disciplined mind from the intellectual.

> [4] *A generation goes, and a generation comes,*
> *but the earth remains forever.*
>
> ECCL 1:4

Qohelet, the wise man, knew that death is both natural and unnatural; he taught contradiction to be at the heart of reality. Up from the ground we have risen only to return, like temporary spirits inhabiting a moment in time, leaving a memory, a story. It is only truth that remains in the unfolding drama of God's history. The aged live to give truth away; the strong live to serve, to learn, and to grow old. The children live to remind us all of an innocence lost. When God was a child, he was like you and I. When we became adults, we failed to be like him. When we are older and the end draws near, look to the children: their testimony is that God lives; there is hope, always hope. Tomorrow's hope is the wise and faithful words of the aged whispered in the ears of a child. Dare to believe that the world, as it is, is not all there is. There is a kingdom where God reigns, an eternal reality of spirit where death loses its grip and we, like children, rise again.

Reading Two

The Childlike Qualities of Jesus People

Shangri-La

Shangri-La has no history.
History is for mortals who measure time in the cycles of death that govern life.
Perennial happiness has no history.
Happiness is, for mortals, the balm that heals the pain of living.
Qohelet, the wise king of Jerusalem, wrote that laughter is madness.
We laugh at the absurd. Perhaps he is right.
Is happiness merely the satisfying of desire?
Is happiness possible without love?
Yet love suffers, weeps, bleeds. Love has a history.
Perhaps love would be unknowable if there were no history?
History in the Jewish tradition began with the birth of desire, desire amiss from relational submission to the being of Love.
In order to be known, love entered history.
Amidst the violence of human history, love offers a path that leads beyond Shangri-La;
a place where joy has a history.

[15] People were bringing even infants to him that he might touch them; and when the disciples saw it, they sternly ordered them not to do it. [16] But Jesus called for them and said, "Let the little children come to me, and do not stop them; for it is to such as these that the kingdom of God belongs. [17] Truly I tell you, whoever does not receive the kingdom of God as a little child will never enter it."

LUKE 18:15–17

Everyday Thoughts

The Childlike Qualities of Jesus People

Jesus teaches that entering the reign of God requires qualities belonging to children. We have all been children, so it is evident in Jesus' statement that we have lost some powers for approaching life—powers we once possessed. First, acknowledging that Jesus is inviting us to consider the healthy aspects of childlike behavior, all unhealthy situations do not qualify as models.

Of course dependency is easily identified as part of a child's life. Entering the reign of God requires trust and faith in God as our father. It is a step of inclusion that embraces others beyond our immediate family. Children recognize we are all children of God. There is a point in childhood when everyone is equal and differences are bridged with kindness, sharing, and friendship. In the economy of children, sharing is an act of loving justice.

Children practice worldmaking through imaginative exercises where they take on characters and live in an alternate world, while ignoring the present. The ability to ignore does not annul the alternate reality of the adult world; however, it exemplifies a power to live in relationship to a worldmaking imagination. As a model, it exemplifies the now/not yet reality of the kingdom of God and it is consistent with a theology of exile. Part of manifesting the kingdom (or reign) of God is to form an alternate reality through a community (an *ecclesia*) that, in a sense, ignores the sociocultural constructs of the larger society. The reign of God does not cater to the culture; rather, it forms a new world—a new reality—a spiritual body of believers, living as persons caught up in Christ Jesus.

> Part of manifesting the kingdom or reign of God is to form an alternate reality through a community (an ecclesia) that, in a sense, ignores the socio-cultural constructs of the larger society.

The imaginative powers of worldmaking belong to the innocence of children and is consistent with the prophets. The imaginative powers of the prophets were rallied to transform the world with calls to justice and righteousness. Jesus' vision of the reign of God is like that of the prophets, but Jesus' teaching announces the reign of God as initiated with the presence of his person, life, and ministry. Jesus' life brings the Spirit of God into the world, into humanity in a way not known by former generations. God is starting over once again; God is giving human beings God's self, God's Spirit, a new covenant—one that fulfills the lack of the earlier covenant.

Imagination has become a spiritual exercise for moving reality toward God. Like the prophets, we are all called to imagine a new world and live in that world right now, ignoring the present world (while paying taxes, and abiding by the laws of society that are acceptable before God). Our goal is the transformation of humanity through the redeeming power of God's Spirit, freely given to all who believe. God's work is redemption, and redemption is the process of salvation worked out in the present. It prepares us for eternity, for life with God.

> Children think original thoughts out of their imagination; original thought is the essence of their inquisitiveness.

The moral imagination of children is reflective of the image of God they bear. The exercise of their moral imagination is the beginning of their spirituality. Children think original thoughts out of their imagination; original thought is the essence of their inquisitiveness. Part of becoming like a child is to escape the boundaries of thought that imprison the imagination to the past, to the established structures of society and culture. It is not enough to imagine a new world; we must, in some sense, reform the present and live out our imagination.

Facing reality, possessing spiritual intelligence is an eye-opening experience that exposes all the error, the violence, and the evil of the present. For an adult to become childlike is not to become ignorant or naive, but to mature and be conformed to the image of God. It is to be like Jesus—to face reality and bring heaven to earth, living in harmony with the redeeming work of God.

Adults must learn to practice their imagination in the face of systemic powers that rule our world. The imagination reworks possibilities not evident to people living in closed systems of power that are dictated by the powerful. The adult imagination imagines training military troops in compassionate aid work so that they can be deployed to help other peoples suffering a natural crisis. The goal of this type of imagination is the subversion of the world; it imagines a day when weapons are exchanged for farming and construction tools (Mic 4:3; Isa 2:4).

Reading Three

Not a Book for Children

Who Speaks for God?

Church is a frightening place
Men and women claim to know God
Claim to speak for God
Excelling in dogma
Failing in grace
Confident in their claims
Ready to destroy any offender of their encultured religious constructs
Church is frightening because people have been schooled in fear
Brought to salvation through fear of hell
Rather than the cross of God's love
God's death at human hands
God's resurrection is the power of God's justice
The hammer of God disables them from contending with their perception of God
Listen to Job; the man who contended with God and spoke truly
His concerns are with justice not with dogma
He knows no confessions or creeds
His sole abiding truth is one God who's justice he cannot find in a world of suffering
Listen to Job; the man who would be hidden in Sheol
Only to await the justice of God to redeem his life
Listen to Job; the voice of humanity
He calls for God to become human
Do you have eyes of flesh? Do you see as humans see?
His answer was hidden, yet to come

The word made flesh, God's son
Storyteller, communicator of compassion
Friend of sinners; he has spoken for God

Not a Book for Children

We are to Worship the Living God, not Words on a Page

You could destroy all the Bibles in the world and the story of Jesus would prevail; God would still speak. We would write again, prophets would speak, the story of Jesus would be preserved. We can never protect the written word by taking life. The gospel cannot be properly carried across the world on the backs of soldiers; even for a nation claiming to be God's chosen. The Bible is not sacred, it is not alive; it is paper, and ink, and often bound with animal flesh. The Bible can become an object of idolatry. The written word is not equivalent to the living word that has resurrected. Jesus said that his sheep hear his voice. Jesus still speaks and there are those that still hear. The world needs those who hear in purity of heart, without pretense or selfish desires for fame.

Jesus would challenge the Bible scholars of his day with words taken from their own book. He would send them back to learn and give them a specific piece of scripture as a lens through which to read.

> [7] *And if you had known what this means,*
> *"I desire mercy, and not sacrifice,'*
> *you would not have condemned the guiltless."*
>
> MATT 12:7

Jesus claims that the teachers of his age did not understand the desire of God for mercy over sacrifice. Jesus was a master at using the scripture, and was not afraid to add his own "but I say to you" when he desired to take the scripture further than what was written.

The Bible is only as Good as the Person Reading it

We are all concerned about the preservation of the text; yet, regardless of what we preserve, each day someone uses the Bible to justify a myriad of errant ideologies and desires. The Bible is not a book for children, nor is it a book for use by anyone who chooses to pick it up. The Bible is a collection of works from an ancient world, long since buried in the sands of time. It is the Spirit behind, in, and even between the lines that brings life to the words and stories that fill the book we regard as our religious text. These words and stories that fill the pages of our book should shock any sensitive heart. Stories of genocide and sacrificing children are not suitable for young kids.

> Truly the Bible is only as good as the person reading it.

It is the teaching of the person who uses the text that is superior to any rules provided by the science of interpretation. Truly the Bible is only as good as the person reading it. The Bible is not a collection of formulas or incantations; it is a book that requires engagement by human beings. The Bible is a limited document in that it does not tell us how to read its many confusing stories and claims. However, there are always plenty of people ready to step forward and claim they know and can explain the tensions we find filling its pages. Kierkegaard would claim that the teacher is greater than the teaching. I agree; Jesus is greater than his teaching. The living Christ is more than the words that form his teaching.

I am guilty; I am one of those persons that claims to have insight into the scriptures. Perhaps we should all take to heart the words of James (I have tried).

> [1] *Let not many of you become teachers, my brethren, for you know that we who teach shall be judged with greater strictness.* [2] *For we all make many mistakes.*
>
> JAS 3:1-2

I am not at a halt to speak about any problem found in the Bible. I can read the text from the vantage point of the many tools afforded me by linguistics, hermeneutics, and so on. I know God is greater than all the tools of learning I've acquired. I also know that God has spoken unequivocally from the cross of Christ. Paul would claim this event as the defining event for all theology, for all revelation. The message of the cross—the story of God crucified as a human being—is the gospel. What does it mean? I am sure it does not mean that God's anger toward sin (and the sinner) required him to torture himself so that he might somehow be able to forgive humanity. John's reading is important for our theology of the cross.

Not a Book for Children

> ¹⁶ *For God so loved the world that he gave his only Son, that whoever believes in him should not perish but have eternal life.* ¹⁷ *For God sent the Son into the world, not to condemn the world, but that the world might be saved through him.*
>
> JOHN 3:16-17

The word "sacrifice" is not used in John's gospel. This is significant for understanding the crucifixion of Jesus. The death of Jesus at the hands of humanity is an act of God's love and self-revelation. Because of the life of Jesus, humanity can be embraced into the Spirit (being) of God.

We all seem compelled to surrender to our personal survival instincts, to a view of the world centered on the self. Jesus surrendered instinct and reasoning. He loved the world from a place he would have preferred to have never gone. Jesus' expressed interpretation of the cross is displayed in his words spoken while being crucified. First is his promise of life to the criminal dying with him, next is the forgiveness of all humanity in his prayer that acknowledges our ignorance; the suffering of God that occurs each time his voice is rejected. The cross is not reasonable; it is not just. Rather, it is God's love spoken loudly to humanity.

> The death of Jesus at the hands of humanity is an act of God's love and self-revelation.

We all are guilty of silencing God's voice in our lives. The Bible teaches that the silencing of a voice is the rejection, even the murder, of a person (note Abel never speaks in the story of the first murder). God's voice surrendered to God's death and the message of the cross cries out across the generations. God will not wage war with humanity; instead, he instructs us through his life lived as a human being. We all need to revisit Paul's hymn on Love's behavior in 1 Corinthians 13. We also need to be reminded of the words of Micah.

> ⁶ *With what shall I come before the LORD, and bow myself before God on high? Shall I come before him with burnt offerings, with calves a year old?* ⁷ *Will the LORD be pleased with thousands of rams, with ten thousands of rivers of oil? Shall I give my first-born for my transgression, the fruit of my body for the sin of my soul?"*
> ⁸ *He has showed you, O man, what is good; and what does the LORD require of you but to do justice, and to love kindness, and to walk humbly with your God?*
>
> MIC 6:6–8

Reading Four

Language Must Always be in Color

Words

Words are like water
you cannot hold them they will slip away
like vapor words rise to reappear in a different form
Words are like the wind
you can feel them
you cannot restrain them
Words are like spirit
they are unpredictable in power
you cannot control them
Words are like a painting
their meaning is in the eye of the listener
Words are like music
they live in the heart

Language is Always Living

This piece offers some thoughts on language. I myself have struggled with the need to use words correctly, to speak with precision, to be understood, to teach my students to avoid or abstain completely from colloquialisms when writing academic papers on interpretation or other disciplines. I must confess I was prompted into this thought by numerous incidents, events, and even some contemporary movies.

Language Must Always be in Color

My thoughts at this point are preliminary to what I hope will become a more extensive reflection on this subject. However, I cannot feign complete ignorance to the subject, for it has possessed my thoughts in different ways and on various occasions. I will use the word "color" as a metaphor for the life of language that defies absolute communication.

It is apparent that the professional disciplines all develop their own terms that denote membership to the guild; perhaps none so much as the legal profession. This is important because the legal profession attempts to develop a precision of language that is unknown in other disciplines where metaphors and stories sit in contrast to the oath-bearing search for truth in courtroom testimony. For example, legal experts reject double negatives in speech, but most of us understand a person's intent free from the legal demands for perfection in speech.

If the color is taken out of language for the sake of linguistically precise communication, then the system that incorporates this practice will become static, absolutist, and evolve towards a totalitarian oligarchy of power. The courtroom, however, is not without its color: the competing attorneys, the power of the judge, and ultimately the color of the jury. The jury, those peers, those common people with their diverse opinions and colloquial colored language of the street, it is in their hands that justice is deemed most likely to be achieved. Language can never be so precise as to ensure absolute communication. Perhaps this is why mathematics, with its emphasis on precision, is referenced as a language—only to fall prey to "chaos theory."

> If the color is taken out of language for the sake of linguistically precise communication, then the system that incorporates this practice will become static, absolutist, and evolve towards a totalitarian oligarchy of power.

Perhaps the ultimate danger in the privatizing of law through mandatory arbitration agreements is the loss of color, the loss of the jury, the problem of absolutist language without the colloquial, without the emotive and passionate use of language where metaphors and the "ya knows" have meaning within a context or culture. The conflicting monetary interest of the authorial powers in the arbitration clause business is an intolerable injustice.

I'm thinking I could replace the word "color" in my previous few thoughts with the word "spirit." This is because although God spoke at creation, no one was there to hear (unless one considers the "us" to address the angels) and although the "word became flesh" it was the flesh that colored

13

Everyday Thoughts

the absolute word clothed in humanity. Even that book we call the word of God is indirect communication, with the simplicity of the Decalogue as close to direct (or precise) communication as we seem to be able to receive.

Perhaps those tongues of fire on the day that the Spirit descended to begin the eschaton ignite the tongue with "spirit" in a way that defies babble and enables hearing. I think hearing the "spirit" of a human being with their poorly constructed linguistic skills, with their colloquial colored speech, their abstract use of metaphor, their language that demands you hear beyond their words, hearing them, defies and challenges the hypocrisy of precise speech.

To view precise speech as superior to the requirement of hearing (people's) words ignores hearing as a spiritual discipline, a reflection of human maturation, it is in effect to worship words and not the God who is spirit, nor the Lord who became flesh. No single soul can control the fluidity of language; language is immune to totalitarianism. Language is alive with humanity, alive with spirit, alive with perspectives from the heart; like God, language cannot be tamed.

> No single soul can control the fluidity of language; language is immune to totalitarianism.

I remember a few decades back the phrase, "ya hear me?" and the response "I hear ya, bro" became popular; as did "do ya feel me?" If ya can't hear me, if ya can't feel me, then you're without the finer attributes of being human that are conducive to spirit.

I remember that the prophets used metaphor, poetry, sign acts, and lived their message with a passion that could ignite the world aflame with different responses that were dependent upon the heart of the ones hearing, observing, and feeling.

God is present in words like redemption, reconciliation, mercy, justice, love, kindness, forgiveness, humility, patience, and those other finer aspects of humanity that exhibit God's image in the world, that put flesh to spirit; those words void of precision, wracked with the potential for pain and suffering, but bearing the hope that carries the world forward with God, with spirit.

Reading Five

Myth and Romanticism

Human Drama and Divine Watching

We human beings are all captivated by the great adventure of God's creative existence; all powerful little creatures, weakened and fearful souls.
Living in the dark night of tension's grip somewhere between despair and hope
The unfolding drama of human life holds the attention of God himself
He rests like a casual observer who has traveled the distance between heaven and us many times
He watches like a helpless father from a distance, waiting and anxious to see what choices his children will make on their journey
The unfathomable portal of death defeated awaits all God's children
Like a final word on existence death demands our attention
Life calls out from a story lived long ago
Life's great secret revealed remains hidden
The simplicity of grace and forgiveness of mercy and love remain the domain of exceptional saints
The human constructed gods of inevitability affirm death's power
Heaven is lost in the world below
God's few witnesses seek the communion of saints and God, ignoring the power of suffering, collective suffering, the suffering of God
Ritual sacrifice is abhorred, social scapegoating appalling
Self-sacrificial love is a heroic virtue revealed on a cross
There is pain in the eyes of the redeemed exiles living below
Smiles lie, laughter mocks, but tears cleanse the soul
A good death dies with a defeated dream

Everyday Thoughts

The blood of martyrs, the seed of life, God rises to watch and honor
Father forgive them for they do not know what they are doing

Myth and Romanticism

The romanticizing of national leaders is a common practice. In this respect, history is kind. However, the purpose for romanticizing national leaders is propaganda for promoting the myth of the state as divine. This nationalist use of romanticism is practiced in biblical interpretation by some, particularly in regards to the figures of David and Solomon. This has caused many to read about David and Solomon with romanticized views and not critique them for their actions or character. Indeed, they are *entitled* to err, their duplicity necessary for the greater good. Thus the basic ethical code that the end is preexistent in the means is violated, along with justice and righteousness.

Romanticism is flawed when a leader is the object; it is an infatuation that erases blemishes and hides glaring evil. The adoration or hope placed in a political figure is like reaching for a messiah; it is idolatry. The myth of their greatness contributes to the ongoing pursuit of another godlike political figure. The political role is not an illusion; it is an effective power that possesses the claim to decide who should live and who should die. It is a power that divides up the resources of the land according to structures of power that tax, conscript for military service, and commandeer the voice of God to justify its policies. It is for this reason that Jesus identifies himself as "son of man" rather than "son of David."

In effect, we carry myths around with us, they are incorporated into our thoughts and senses. So people versed in the biblical narratives carry around David and Solomon, the father-and-son team, the myth of royalty, the myth of the hero and the wise man, the myth of the persons greater than ourselves, whose work and legacy cannot be undone or questioned.

For instance, when reading David's refusal to take the life of Saul, a feeling of rightness accompanies David's actions. His respect for the position of Saul is often received as a profound act of character. Yet, the portrayal of David in Samuel should lead us to recognize that David's genius as a master propagandist is at play. One day David will be king and Saul's followers must become David's. Further, if Saul's life is too sacred to be taken (for David has no qualms about killing, whether innocent or guilty), then David's life will also

> In effect we carry myths around with us, they are incorporated into our thoughts and senses.

Myth and Romanticism

be sacred. On the one hand, David is ensuring a long life for himself. On the other hand, we see how in the development of nation-states the assassination of the king or president is taboo. You cannot take the leader's place through killing them because you remove the myth of sacredness from their person and put your own life at risk when you take their place (at least you do not want to be caught for being the one responsible).

When reading the story of Solomon's wisdom (1 Kgs 3), the romantic view dominates. Typically he is a man of wisdom and his threat to butcher a child was merely to get at the truth and could not possibly have been carried out; the end justifies the means. All wisdom seems to vanish when people read this story; for wisdom is discovered in refusing the story's surface attribution of wisdom to the demagogue Solomon. Questions should fill the reader's mind. Why is this story located at this point in the book of Kings? If you want to exhibit the grand wisdom of a great king, is this the kind of example you want to offer? Wouldn't some great feat of engineering that brought irrigation to the land be superior? Wouldn't some discovery of a biological nature that defeated a chronic disease be a better example? That the entire nation was fed and educated would surely be an indication of wisdom in a great king.

Unfortunately, we receive this story as a positive lesson rather than as a picture of a king whose reign produces abuse and despair in women. One of the women was so distraught that she took the life of her child. The other, still hopeful, appears before the king and exhibits greater wisdom than the king through her words and actions. The story reveals that Solomon's wisdom is centered on executing justice (on babies, no less!). Solomon's kingdom of gold is bought at the expense of mercy and justice—the death of the innocent. The story should have the effect of bringing the reader to tears at the condition of society in Solomon's time and at the hard heart of the foolish wise man. It seems that the reason we receive the piece as it is written is because some scribe had to cover his intentions with a subversive story, like Nathan's parable delivered to David. People are prone to a legal reading of the story rather than a compassionate reading. The worship of law as a solution to social problems becomes a license for ignoring the finer aspects of being human, like compassion, mercy, and responsibility for the poor.

The Psalms add to our romanticism of David due to the many attributions of Davidic authorship. However, if we make the move to read these attributions as dependent upon the romanticized view of David as the archetype for the nation, then we have a less than subtle move to replace Abraham

17

with David. Who is the father of Israel as a nation: Abraham or King David? Does David's covenant compete with Abraham's? Does Mt. Zion compete with Moriah? Who is greater: The man of faith or the man of violence?

The Psalter is a book of songs filled with nationalism, yet it offers insight into human behavior and expresses humanity's voice addressed to God. When read as a collection, the Psalter reveals the history of Israel and is rich with theology for the discerning reader. When we understand that the Psalter wrestles with the presence of nationalism in its compositions, we can recognize the power of nationalism as an idol able to permeate religious expression. The Psalter is much richer than I have delineated in this paragraph and requires a level of maturity and intelligence for reading. It is distressing that Christians have reduced this rich theological resource to a book for selective reading in order to feel good.

This tendency of nationalism to enter the songs of religious expression and worship can be seen in a modern composition taken from a piece of Chronicles. I do not sing "Our God is Greater" when I hear it used by a music leader. This is because we believe in one God, so there is no god for the one God to be greater than. The song contributes to polytheism and likely the piece of scripture it is taken from reflects Israel's gradual acceptance of monotheism. Besides, when I, as a modern in the twenty-first century, sing this song, do I suppose I must shout at others and say my God is greater than your god? All this will do is bring animosity into the world. Isn't it better to be a blessing and help people find God by being able to communicate with them, meet them where they are? There is no humility in such a song.

It is the revelation of monotheism that changes all religious claims and it is the particularity of Christian faith in Jesus Christ as Lord that we celebrate. It is the revelation of God in the man Jesus Christ that makes Christianity a non-combative faith inviting all humanity to good news (not nationalist competition). If we truly know God, then meeting others with grace and love is the way, not shouts of superiority. Besides, this kind of statement builds the arrogance of an individual more than it blesses the one God. Sometimes those Gentiles are closer to the truth than we are; like that centurion—that Roman oppressor of the people of God—that heathen polytheist who understood the authority of a simple peasant named Jesus (Matt 8:5–13). We need to sing God is greater than our hearts (1 John 3:20).

> To read compassionately is to remember the poor, the suffering, the victims of our wars and greed, of our failure to live in accordance with the teachings of scripture.

Myth and Romanticism

> [9] *The heart is deceitful above all things,*
> *And desperately wicked;*
> *Who can know it?*
>
> JER 17:9

I think Jeremiah's contemplative remarks on the human heart reflect the constant barrage of choices and possibilities that we as human beings entertain in our thoughts. Also, the human propensity for evil is always shocking. The Lord tests the heart and searches the emotions. It seems that even the Lord is surprised by the capacity of human beings to do evil (Jer 3:7, 19).

> [20] *For if our heart condemns us, God is greater than our heart, and knows all things.*
>
> 1 JOHN 3:20

In general, the romanticism of scripture in its entirety is reductionist and removes intellect, wisdom, insight, and meaning from the text. I do not advocate removing the heart from reading, but the heart needs to be used in a compassionate way when reading, not a romantic way. To read compassionately is to remember the poor, the suffering, the victims of our wars, greed, and failure to live in accordance with the teachings of scripture. We must learn to read critically with faith and compassion that we might not fall prey to the nationalism, militarism, and materialism that fills the hearts of the masses—the crowd.

Reading Six

Absolute Love Demonstrated in Human Beings

O God, Watcher of Humanity

O God, watcher of humanity, as you view the unfolding life of the passing generations, do you lean forward, captivated, gripped in compassion, admiration, as suffering human beings display immovable love and faith? Surely, O Lord, all your heart is with the righteous who suffer and in their suffering display love.

O God, father of humanity, do you weep when a little one is broken and wasted under the tyranny of hubris—human cruelty? Surely you gather up and embrace the righteous soul who did not know your name.

Where is the man, the woman that speaks for God? Are their voices silenced by the blind powers whose voices fill the earth? Are not the greatest stories those of human nobility birthed and held in suffering? O Lord are you the God of suffering or the suffering God?

Should not the man, the woman that dares to speak for God enter into the suffering of humanity? Where is the voice of God but with the cries of the poor and captive masses? Where is the attention of God but on the noble sufferer?

O God, conflicted with tears and joy, you watch as the oppressed soul finds you in their suffering and defies the world with faith. Where is the man or woman who proclaims the message, Jesus' gospel of God's reign? Surely they are not found courting celebrities, politicians, or military officials; surely they are not found wearing gold or with many houses; surely they are not those that make agreements with the violent and justify injustice. They cannot speak for you because they do not know where to find you.

Absolute Love Demonstrated in Human Beings

My son and students often said I delivered submarine sandwiches in the form of purposefully articulated statements that comprised lots of thought, an idea, a way of thinking about God and the world. The following is one of those statements.

Human reality is so fraught with uncertainty that the sole evidence of an absolute in the human family is the formation of an immovable character expressing agape *in the face of suffering and death. It is the existential moment of tragedy and spirit where we enter the suffering of Christ and imagine God with the frightening clarity of the cross.*

Each person experiences human reality differently. Although there are constants related to our biological needs and consistency in the natural world, there is unpredictability in nature, in relationships, in the fragility of life. This uncertain part of our existence holds possibility for both good and evil. It is the negative part of uncertainty that drives us to secure ourselves against the hostility of the world. The positive aspect of uncertainty is the open possibility for good.

However, east of Eden, in the land of wandering, we seek to find our way in a world where good and evil become so enmeshed that separation seems to be a task only God can accomplish. So the two exist together (for now). It is for this reason that grace and forgiveness are to be constants in life as we press together for the good.

> [29] But he replied, "No; for in gathering the weeds you would uproot the wheat along with them."
>
> MATT 13:29

Uncertainty is the tragic, the uncontrollable aspects of life lived under the sun. To say that human reality is fraught with uncertainty is to acknowledge that all of us, no matter how saintly, experience some concern over the possibility for evil, for the tragic to disrupt

> In the reality of being human, is there an absolute?

our lives. This is because none of us escapes the powers of evil and the disruption of the tragic.

> [13] Come now, you who say, "Today or tomorrow we will go to such and such a town and spend a year there, doing business and making money." [14] Yet you do not even know what tomorrow will bring. What is your life? For you are a mist that appears for a little while and then vanishes. [15] Instead you ought to say, "If the Lord wishes, we will live and do this or that." [16] As it is, you boast in your arrogance; all such boasting is evil. [17] Anyone, then, who knows the right thing to do and fails to do it, commits sin.
>
> JAS 4:13–17

I am attempting to identify a lived moment when certainty is experienced and portrayed in such a way that it is indicative of an absolute power (Spirit) residing within a human being. James contrasts uncertainty with a willingness to do what is right. James concludes that living in a manner that ignores the unexpected is evil, and that living every moment with a willingness to respond by doing good is the wisdom of faith. This kind of attitude towards the present enables a person to live with openness to the unpredictable in humanity, nature, and God. The spiritual maturity expressed in openness to uncertainty on a daily basis is essential for ongoing character formation.

The uncertainty that we face is not always pleasant or good; rather, most often, it is tragic and evil. Human reality does not function in a healthy way without love, and love functions through grace and forgiveness, through acts of kindness that enable other human beings to flourish. These are not mere niceties but promote creation in the realm of the human. In contrast, the constant securing of one's life with wealth and power, and doing so without concern for others or the created world, is anxiety's response to uncertainty, resulting in evil.

The person that connects fully with the divine love is able to rest without the race for security at the expense of others. It is this connection with God that lifts a human being above the fear of suffering and death, not like a warrior that surrenders to the inevitable, but like a martyr who reveals God in their death.

I have suggested in my italicized statement in the second paragraph of this essay that to love with the power of the divine (Greek: *agape*, or Hebrew: *hesed*) in the presence of suffering and death is evidence of an absolute—a moment when certainty is attained, when love prevails over suffering and death by refusing to live in a way contrary to the formation of character.

In my writing, for a number of years, I have used the word absolute only twice. The statement under scrutiny is one of those times. The following is the other time.

There is meaning to life because God, who is watching, cares deeply about how we live. This does not alleviate the reality of suffering. Indeed, I am convinced that suffering and death prepare us for absolute dependency upon God throughout the ages.

So, we will one day be in a position before God of absolute dependency, able to resist the power of illicit and unhealthy desire. In the present, this position of absolute dependency is viewable in the lives of people that embrace the suffering of others as their own; these few souls are not free from struggle, yet in their lives we recognize a capacity for virtue that surpasses most all of us.

Suffering and tragedy cannot be escaped, but they can be overcome by love. In the life of Jesus, this existential moment of tragedy, and spirit-formed character, are viewed in Jesus' words when he prayed for his murderers to be forgiven for their actions. He even excuses them for being ignorant. This is the frightening element of the cross. Since in Christ the one God suffered tragedy and death, we also must learn to embrace that from which we spend so much effort attempting to escape by securing our way in the world with wealth and power. We must embrace tragedy, injustice, and suffering with an immovable love that exhibits the power of an absolute—the love of God for every human being.

The cross is the pathway to resurrection. This is not to say that we must all become martyrs or die at the hands of others in order to obtain the resurrection. Rather, it is to point out with clarity that a fully formed human being will endure suffering with love. It is the moment of grace when love and spirit are seen with clarity—when all angst, hate, anger, and self-preservation are captured up in dependency on God. It

> This moment is the display of immovable character, not even the finality of death can inhibit the certainty displayed with absolute conviction.

is the display of absolute dependency in the present with the most convincing proof: an unconquerable love in the grips of evil. This moment is the display of immovable character; not even the finality of death can inhibit the certainty displayed with absolute conviction.

> [54] *Now when the centurion and those with him, who were keeping watch over Jesus, saw the earthquake and what took place, they were terrified and said, "Truly this man was God's Son!"*
>
> Matt 27:54

 The manner in which Jesus died brought the presence of God into the realm of death; the earth shook and death could not hold this man who died with an immovable character, faithfully expressing the love of God. He commended his spirit to God and breathed his last, entering the realm of the unknowable and the unsustainable—the absence of God.

 We human beings are surrounded by death, pain, and suffering. It is the divine love reigning in our hearts that overcomes the world. The love of God never gives up; it is eternal, absolute. It is put on display in the cross of Jesus, in the life of non-violent martyrs; it is the power that conquers death and births resurrection into the world.

Reading Seven

Christianity: The Cure for Human Hubris

The Philippian Hymn

The Descent

> Let the same mind be in you that was in Christ Jesus,
> who, though he was in the form of God,
> did not regard equality with God as something to be exploited,
> but emptied himself,
> taking the form of a slave,
> being born in human likeness.
> And being found in human form,
> he humbled himself and became obedient to the point of death
> even death on a cross.

The Ascent

> Therefore God also highly exalted him
> and gave him the name that is above every name,
> so that at the name of Jesus every knee should bend,
> in heaven and on earth and under the earth,
> and every tongue should confess that Jesus Christ is Lord,
> to the glory of God the Father.

PHIL 2:5–11

Christianity: The Cure for Hubris

The Hymn of Christ in Paul's epistle to the Philippian church is a prime piece of scripture that attests to the continual need for human beings to choose a servant role over constructs of power. Paul is writing to a group of people that seem to be free from the problems he addresses in his epistles to other churches. I am using the hymn as instructive to cure hubris in the church, a cure that can generate healing in a world fractured by the violence of hubris.

Whether this piece of scripture ever formed the lyrics of a theologically rich hymn sung by the first-century church is not my concern in this essay. I like to think that it did, and that young songwriters might become aware of the importance of Christ-centered theology in lyrics.

Paul admonishes the Philippians to develop a way of thinking that is consistent with the model of Jesus' self-emptying and obedience to God. The example seems extreme in light of Jesus' identity as LORD. How can we follow? Yet, Jesus was one of us: flesh and blood, a human being. Although we are called to follow by the one that descended from heaven, his model was accomplished as a human being. This makes our need to conform to the 'mind' of Jesus portrayed in the Philippian hymn a religious conviction of ultimate concern.

Hubris is easily brought to the surface of our personality through the necessary function of assertiveness. The expression of human personality through words and actions requires some degree of assertiveness in a world of relationships. We do not encounter Jesus as a non-assertive personality, yet the Philippian hymn seems to counter self-assertive behavior.

At issue then is how self-assertiveness is to be lived out in light of the call to humility and obedience. This call is the way of Jesus. It is an ideology that Jesus held to while affirming truth and challenging injustice. It is evident that Jesus lived and taught without the structural tools of authority that maintain power through coercion and force. Further, it is evident that Jesus refused to sanction any form of violence as a compatible tool for supporting his teaching.

Jesus' self-assertiveness is not for the success of his person, but for the proclamation of truth. Jesus' acts of self-assertion are for the healing, deliverance, and maturation of others into the fullness of humanity. Jesus is the consummate servant, serving both God and humanity. Christianity is a religion and calls us to a life of meaning beyond the temporal present into the age to come. For this reason, the extreme call to follow Jesus into a life of self-effacing, as displayed in the Philippian hymn, is more than a philosophy. It is the recognition of the emergence of God into the world through the followers of the Lord Jesus Christ.

> [8] *he humbled himself and became obedient to the point of death— even death on a cross.*
>
> PHIL 2:8

> [24] *For those who want to save their life will lose it, and those who lose their life for my sake will save it.*
>
> LUKE 9:24

The initial temptation to succumb to the power of hubris is the will to survive at the expense of another. Jesus' way of humility through serving others is the death knell of hubris. If we are to live in the way of Jesus we must learn to combat our personal hubris while affirming assertiveness that represents truth and liberates the oppressed.

> As an enterprise of the Spirit, accomplished through those that follow Jesus, God's emergence into the world is accomplished through saints that, like Jesus, lose their lives.

Personal hubris is the failure to hear the voice of another and listen. I believe we are called to be disciples of listening to God. God listens to the cries of the poor and oppressed, so we should cultivate the skill of listening to others, particularly the suffering. Only through hearing the other can we develop a real empathy that expresses love rather than pity.

Jesus calls us not only to love the needy, but also to love our enemies, even those demonized by our nation-state. When we do not love our enemies then we become enemies of God. We are able to love our enemies because we know that death does not have the final word on our existence, because God loves and redeems. We know this because in response to the way of Jesus, God raised him from the dead and seated him at God's side of equality.

Reading Eight

Called to Renounce Violence

World Dreaming

I dream of a world where soldiers train only to respond to natural disasters,
to save lives and rebuild homes and roads
I dream of a world where schools teach children the value of becoming a moral human being
I dream of a world where the acquisition of wealth for personal aggrandizement no longer exists
I dream of a world without celebrities,
a world where every person is valued
I dream of a world where peace is taught and violence forgotten
I dream of a world where efforts at space exploration are seen as folly
for we have failed to end war and poverty caused by national powers
I dream of a world where the elderly are not forgotten but sought out for their wisdom.
I dream of a world of grace and merciful redeeming justice
I would that we all dream of such a world
It is the world to come, it is the coming of God in humanity
It is the kingdom come as we have been taught to pray for by our Lord Jesus

Nonviolence a Calling

Although nonviolence is an ethical value, my pursuit in this piece is to provide an understanding of the living ethic that enables a person to live a nonviolent life. As an ethic, nonviolence in popular thought is currently placed outside

Called to Renounce Violence

the context of normalcy and is viewed either as a purely religious conviction, or an impractical ideal that ignores the harsh realities of human life. Simply put, human beings are violent and violence is viewed as an unalterable fact of the human condition. Christianity calls humanity away from violence and through the Spirit of the Lord we are enabled to become nonviolent persons.

The Hebrew people developed a plethora of interesting perspectives on human violence in the Old Testament. I will begin with a brief look at one perspectival claim in order to establish the relation of God to human violence. The flood story is first a response to the flood stories of the ancient Near Eastern world; it is to be understood as a polemic that rejects ancient Near Eastern cosmologies, while establishing the theology of the Hebrews. It is this Hebraic theology that I am interested in for establishing the relation of God to human violence.

A common theological theme in the Hebrew Scriptures is that the ethical and moral behavior of humanity affects the ground (even the cosmos). The first evidence of this idea is in the garden story where the human condition generates the existence of thorns and thistles. Further, this theological concept is easily established by a simple cursory reading of a couple of scriptures.

> [14] *If my people who are called by my name humble themselves, pray, seek my face, and turn from their wicked ways, then I will hear from heaven, and will forgive their sin and heal their land.*
>
> 2 Chr 7:14

> [2] *Swearing, lying, and murder, and stealing and adultery break out; bloodshed follows bloodshed.* [3] *Therefore the land mourns, and all who live in it languish; together with the wild animals and the birds of the air, even the fish of the sea are perishing.*
>
> Hos 4:2–3

In the flood story we see that the cause of the flood (*mabbul*) is the violence of humanity. Specifically this violence is depicted in chapter six, where groups of aged men use their longevity to control others and attempt to breed humanity through selecting and taking many wives. The word *mabbul* is used only in this flood narrative and references a return to the primeval waters of chaos in Genesis 1. The cause of the flood is human violence and the response of creation is an upheaval of chaos. God, as the one who designed creation, is the power behind the entire event.

I think we are to focus on the theme of violence that has filled these early narratives if we are to produce healthy theological understanding. As I wrote earlier, the flood story is first a response to earlier flood stories in the surrounding cultures. Secondly, it is a polemic that challenged their cosmologies, which claimed the activity of gods behind the forces of nature. Finally, it is an example of the Hebrews doing theology in narrative form to reveal their God. With these thoughts in mind then it is not the flood that is to draw our attention, but the relation of God, creation, and humanity to the violence that is part of the human condition.

God placed a multi-colored bow of peace in the sky. God's bow placed downward is a symbol, like a man in the ancient Near East placing his bow downward when entering a tent in peace (rather than upright to preserve the bow string). Humanity need not fear a return to *mabbul*; God promises seasons and by his grace allows human beings to live and prosper in spite of their violence. This is the message of the flood story.

The displeasure of God with human violence is revealed in mortality—in the difficulty humanity faces in a world that is not like the garden of God, but rather one capable of natural catastrophe and great harm. The flood story teaches us that humanity's violence is not accepted as compatible with God's will or desire. Rather, God's grace allows humanity to thrive in spite of their violence.

The flood story calls us to reject the violence depicted in the early chapters of Genesis. We are called to accept our creaturely limits and not use our powers of dominion over the creation to commit violence. We are to reject the desire that drives us to kill our brothers and sisters in an effort to establish one culture over another. We are to reject the violence of taking many wives, of attempting to breed humanity (the temptation of genetic science). God is a being of grace and peace; he is not at war with humanity.

> God's grace allows human beings to live in spite of their violence; this is the message of the flood story.

Violence is not to be normalized but identified at its most subtle levels and rejected. Violence is at odds with creation and incompatible with God. Unfortunately, we are all guilty of reaching for the fruit that represents trespassing creaturely limits. When our powers of dominion bring harm to human beings then we have trespassed and partaken from the fruit of the tree of the knowledge of good and evil. Sin is always an act of violence.

Called to Renounce Violence

What is the ethic that enables a person to live a nonviolent life? In a world where violence is only a reach away, how are we to live?

Sensitivity to evil is equivalent with sensitivity to violence. A person with this kind of insight does not fit well in the world in which we live. Such a person becomes like a foreigner, an alien whose cultural ideals are inconsistent with a world of technique, capitalism, limitless science, and any kind of weapon formed to kill human beings. Such a person views humanity as one—as all brothers and sisters—and seeks only to serve for the betterment of human existence, without harming anyone or abusing the creation. It is an error to equate nonviolence with passivity. Rather, in the present age it is a resistant power and can be aggressive without causing harm.

The ethic of nonviolence is embodied in a person who values nonviolence over his or her own life. Their being is resting in their conviction that a life lived free of violence is capable of releasing the power of God into the world. This calling to nonviolence that reaches this deeply into the soul of a human being is a demonstration of a "new creature," of a new birth, of someone that has become "spirit" and is "in the world but not of the world." The person arrested by the call to nonviolence lives each moment valuing a life lived in concert with the Spirit and free of violence over the preservation of their own life.

Such a person, like Jesus, may be called to the place where the giving of their life in an act of nonviolent resistance (an act of love) becomes a specified moment, an hour, and a sign to the world. These are the martyrs of faith, whose lives brought heaven to earth.

It is difficult for me to grasp how any creed or confession that was formed by theologians after the revelation of God in Christ Jesus, would not include the renunciation of violence as essential for the person that would be conformed to the image of God's son. Nonviolence is spirituality. It is a calling, a calling to all of us and for some even to give up their lives. Such souls have touched heaven, have felt the power of eternal life, have seen the face of God.

> The person arrested by the call to nonviolence lives each moment valuing a life lived in concert with the Spirit and free of violence over the preservation of their own life.

God's calling to all humanity and particularly to believers is a path to nonviolent living. God's relation to violence in the world is grace, because human beings are violent. To see and enter the kingdom of God is to become a "new creation," a person whose soul rejects all violence, all evil, and wrestles with remaining in a position before God that is spiritual; not of this world but in the world as flesh.

Reading Nine

Faith and Doubt

Caught in a Paradox

Caught in the Paradox of Life
Struggling to live
while Living without Struggle
Thankful for Simplicity's Smile
Somewhere between Joy and Sorrow
In the Midst of Laughter and Tears
Life's Struggle is Overcome in Her Smile of Grace

Faith and Doubt

We all like to think that doubt and faith are compatible, simply because at some time or another we all experience the human tendency to doubt. Doubt is not necessarily a negative trait; for without doubt we could not question existing claims about our reality or the physical world. Doubt in a sense can reflect the desire of human intellect to exercise insight into accepted norms of thought, and in so doing discover error and gain new understanding or knowledge. Doubt then is not always a negative trait but can serve to keep us safe in a world of inconsistency and surprises. In effect, all philosophy begins with doubt, because to doubt is to question. Without questions, philosophy cannot function.

Faith is a relational word when we are applying it to a proper religious use that denotes belief in God. This being said, faith is a connective, a conduit for spirit between the seen and the unseen. Further, faith requires an object and God is the object of faith. It is an error to have faith in a particular desire to attain something or receive something; faith must be seated in relationship with God so that it is not presumptuous, so that it does not become simply a tool for the individual to attain his/her will. Speaking in faith then is to speak out of our relationship with God, in the spirit; it is God that moves mountains, not us.

Faith is not an individual human being's power; it is the flowing of relationship between God and the believer. So, faith can bring the power of God into the world, but it is his power, not ours. To have faith in the power of God requires understanding how God works in the world; God—and not the acquisition of power—must remain the object of faith. It is written that whatsoever is not of faith is sin.

> [23] *And he that doubteth is damned if he eat, because he eateth not of faith: for whatsoever is not of faith is sin.*
>
> ROM 14:23

In both 1 Corinthians 8 and Romans 14, Paul addresses an interesting subject on sin as a position of the conscience rather than an act. In both cases, to eat meat offered to idols is not a sin. However, to eat this same meat with the inner conviction that to do so is a sin, results in sin. The conscience is wrong to identify the eating of the meat as a sin, but to violate the conscience results in sin, because faith is broken and thus relationship is broken. Faith is to live with the awareness that God is watching; he is present. If a person acts on that which he thinks is sin—even if the act is not sin—he commits a sin because he exercises the will to violate relationship with God. Sin then is not an act but a position before God. It is a position of the will to attain its desire, regardless of whether that desire is consistent with their relationship with God.

In the Christian culture of holiness, sin has been understood to be an act or a thought inconsistent with God's nature. This is true, but needs to be expanded to understand that before the act or thought is accomplished, the heart has already chosen to separate itself from the practice of faith. Faith is not a moment but a consistency of relationship. Faith is a position before God, and even when we are in a position of sin, God's grace can still cover our lives with love. Sin is not an act but a positioning of the conscience before God, a positioning that chooses the self's (ego's) desire over God's will.

Faith as a relational word allows us to understand that not keeping a caring awareness of God at the center of your thoughts, at all times, is sin. Likewise, to keep God in your thoughts and yet violate his nature (holiness) is sin. We grow in faith because we grow in relationship.

In Matthew's story of the centurion's great faith, the centurion recognizes God's authority as present in all places and not dependent upon the presence of Jesus. Likewise the centurion recognized the authority resident in Jesus as a teacher and a prophet, as a person of faith, a person in relationship with God.

It is my assertion that faith and doubt are incompatible if doubt's object is God. Since faith's object is always God, doubt and faith are incompatible. You cannot have hope for receiving something from God unless you first have a living relationship with God.

I am indebted to Kierkegaard for many of my thoughts and terms in this piece.

Reading Ten

Reflections on the Disposition of Sorrow and Joy

The Blues

Learning to live with sorrow
Finding release in lyrics and song
Life rains blue, washes sorrow across the soul
How could I lose you?
Your life is gone
My memory goes on
I've lost myself in a dream
Tenderness holds me captive
Tears have become my friends
Hope holds my hand
Faith reminds me of how you began
Will this sweetness die?
Perhaps it will live forever
I don't know why
Will I drown in tears?
Will tears wash away the loss?
Sweet sorrow makes me know I'm alive

Holding Hands with Both Sorrow and Joy

The human capacity to turn sorrow into sweetness begins with tears. Blues songs, in a sense, celebrate sorrow as a sweet reality that can only be resolved through a memory held in the beauty of music. The loss of gospel lament to the feel-good ditty of this generation's praise songs is to replace facing reality with illusion, even illusory religion. Spirituality faces reality and asks the forbidden questions of religion governed by absolutist ideologies. Spirituality weeps along with the God who weeps.

Trauma

There is sorrow borne of trauma that cannot be turned into sweetness, it can only be tempered through a cathartic experience that is equated with religious experience. Then it must find an outlet in the aesthetic—like writing or poetry or art—and this must be mixed with a maturing faith or it becomes self-destructive.

Trauma is an assault upon the psyche that removes a person's trust in the existence of *goodness* in other human beings, even in God. Tender souls can be lost to the effects of trauma and lose the ability to make good judgments. Without attentiveness to the reality of human suffering in religious practices, trauma victims are alone and isolated from more fortunate persons. A theology of suffering, not as a martyr, but simply as a human being, is essential for a group of believers if they are to help the victim(s) of trauma. Feel-good religion leaves the broken to suffer alone.

Trauma victims hide the pain of sorrow with a smile.

Sorrow holds precious memories that cannot be lost, or horrific memories that must be healed. Healing is not miraculous for the sufferer hurt by inhumane acts, scarred by neglect, wounded by assault, and forgotten by God (a very real feeling for victims of the world's cruelty). Sometimes healing cannot be found and I think that it is either because of damage done to the brain, an inadequate response by the body of Christ, or that God leaves us (humanity) to witness the horror of a life lost to trauma. Human cruelty cannot be erased; its effects are real and strike at us from the life of the broken.

The systems of power that bring violence into the world are exposed in the pain of a human life lost to the effects of trauma. Our sorrow over the often irreparable damage inflicted upon human beings is meant to move us to challenge the systems of power that cause this intolerable harm to the human family. Joy comes from letting the pain of loss move us to resistance while also causing us to exercise open articulation against these powers in every manner possible.

The Sweetness of Sorrow

For the rest of us, our sorrow seeks comfort, seeks an outlet, while (often) containing precious memories for which we are grateful. So, sorrow and joy, laughter and tears, love and loss, all remain alive in us, ready to burst forth in emotions we hold dear.

In this mixture of events, both joyful and painful, is formed our need for meaning. The temporary relief of the aesthetic leaves us seeking to understand the brokenness of our reality, of our lives; it is this need that brings us to God. We come to God out of need; people without need do not need God.

It is God who answers the pain and suffering of our existence with boundless love, love that comforts us with hope for a someday when everything is gonna be alright. Faith that everything is gonna be alright is a denial of our temporal condition. It is a hope for the correcting of all that we do not understand, for healing all the pain and suffering we experience. It is a redemptive reversal of our broken reality that we seek through the sweetness of sorrow.

If we are to live and survive this sad reality then we must learn to live with brokenness. Denial of the impact of loss, tragedy, and illness inhibits spiritual growth and causes dysfunctional living. Living with brokenness requires the glorious gift of our ability to start over, to begin again, to live and hold dear both sorrow and joy. Without brokenness, maturation, even conformity to the Spirit of Christ, is lost. Integration of brokenness into one's spirituality produces humility, and humility cannot exist in a person who resists brokenness with pride or violence. Only love and forgiveness—forgiveness of self, of God, of others—can make possible a healthy human being who loves God and others.

Loss of life, of one's former self, through tragedy or sickness, requires a person to start over, lest they become stuck in a reality that has become either a memory or a dream. Starting over is not running from pain and suffering it is the graceful acceptance of pain and suffering as paradoxically enriching. A matured human being knows there is no expectation for life that can be considered normal; normalcy is a cultural myth that inhibits life. In order to live, to be healthy, concepts of normalcy are responded to with laughter by a matured person.

In the sweetness of sorrow hope lives.

Sorrow makes us human but joy is evidence of our origins as creatures born for the eternal. The dispositions of sweetness and sorrow, as blended emotions, hold us in two worlds and are indicative of our life as flesh and spirit. This perishing, dying flesh, longing for life but captured in the moment, cannot endure without the concept of prevailing goodness. Spirituality is empowering, enabling us to accept reality with grace and wisdom, to turn sorrow into joy, loss into new life, to be born again.

We are made to move towards the reign of God where the Lord wipes away tears while memories remain. The healing of memories will take place as the Lord walks us back through the events of our lives. Some will weep as the one who sinned against them also weeps, and does so before the Lord while seeking forgiveness. However, not just forgiveness from the Lord, but also forgiveness from their victim for the suffering they have caused. In the end, love wins. God, the great lover of humanity, will reconcile his bride to himself in the Lord Jesus.

Reading Eleven

Flesh from the Earth and Glory from Above

My Spiritual Journey

Like an old sage I confronted the dialectical wall of eternity containing the words of the wise and laughed for I knew God was on the other side.
Like a man with a revelation I have known God
Like a wayfaring stranger I have wandered the path of an exile
Like an insignificant soul determined to be true I have faced life with God watching
Like one loved of God I have been encouraged to wrestle the shadows of death while still alive
If laughter is madness then it is good to be free from the constraints of the mind and open to the life of the spirit.
I care not what others think, I have learned the crowd is continually erring
I wait now for my soul to soar far above the minuscule concerns of desire
If I come crashing down I know I will rise again
I long only to be named as one of his children that pleased him

Flesh from the Earth and Glory from Above

I grew up singing, "He hideth my soul in the cleft of a rock." It is a great song and whenever we sang it I thought of Moses tucked away in a crevice, watching God moving away from him, his hand covering the old man at the moment when he was closest.

> [22] *and while my glory passes by I will put you in a cleft of the rock, and I will cover you with my hand until I have passed by;* [23] *then I will take away my hand, and you shall see my back; but my face shall not be seen.*
>
> EXOD 33:22-23

Moses has pleaded with God to see his glory. God has conceded and Moses is to experience him in an unparalleled encounter between the human and the divine. The man Moses will not be "lost" in God; rather, God will not lose Moses. The riches of knowing God, of experiencing God's glory and learning God's ways, will be kept in an earthen treasure of human flesh. God speaks with Moses, Moses speaks with God, and Moses lives. God does not consume; the distinctive personality of Moses in all his limitations is kept, and Moses remains human. Moses has appeared in the presence of God without shoes, in the safety of a fire that would not even consume a bush. God has come near. God is not distant; he's not a mythical power of the cosmos. God is seeking a people and desires to be known.

> [19] *And he said, "I will make all my goodness pass before you."*
>
> EXOD 33:19

In the unfolding narrative, goodness is equated with glory. Moses is going to have an encounter with God of deep spiritual communion; however, intimacy with the divine has limits. In the text the revelation is anthropomorphic: God is pictured as appearing in a human body. However, Moses is prohibited from viewing God's face. This is problematic due to the claim in verse eleven which precedes the event at the end of chapter 33.

> [11] *Thus the LORD used to speak to Moses face to face, as a man speaks to his friend.*
>
> EXOD 33:11

The apparent discrepancy is to alert the reader to the limits of language when communicating the revelation of God in which Moses is to partake. The narrator is not clear on precisely when this revelation took place. It appears that the revelation begins in Exodus 34:5 on the following morning, because God has said he will proclaim his name before Moses, which begins in 34:5.

In spite of the limits of language, the text in its picturesque encounter of God and Moses is instructive. God is pictured as "more than"—more than Moses can comprehend. In the text, Moses' request was to be shown God's way (34:13), which is equivalent to God's glory, which is then defined as God's goodness. Moses wants to know God in such a deeply intimate way that God would become predictable. However, God is always more than, and is to remain incomprehensible and unpredictable regardless of the depth of intimacy that any person is granted.

In the revelatory scene, God is viewed from behind. The implication: God is to be followed; he leads the way. God is living creative movement and we are always in pursuit. Moses' nearness to encountering God in a moment of intimacy is limited by God's hand hiding Moses. Human beings are not capable of knowing God in a way that makes him predictable. There are limits on intimacy with God, limits established for our sake. God can never be so described or so theologically constructed as to become a static entity whose ways fit the limits of human understanding.

> God is alive, the source of life. God is wonderfully free, unpredictably engaged in creation, and refuses to be known in such a way that surprise is removed from our relationship with him.

Life demands the "yes" to God, the yes of love that responds to the relational complexity of human life. Knowing God is a living relationship that requires the yes to God, the yes of love functions irrationally, sacrificially, all in response to the Spirit. Moses wants all of God that he can have!

God is alive, the source of life. God is wonderfully free, unpredictably engaged in creation, and refuses to be known in such a way that surprise is removed from our relationship with him. God is omnific and yet will not be imprisoned by our concept of omnific attributes. For example, perhaps God can literally choose to forget. Theology would argue around God's capacity to forget and deprive him of being able to forget. Theology would imprison God to omniscience and limit God's omnipotence to control his self.

Moses lived in an era of God's unfolding revelation in which the consummate revelatory act of God had not yet been accomplished: Jesus—his life, teaching, death, and resurrection. The experience of glory seems to denote nearness to God that counters the temporary affliction of our mortality (2 Cor 4:16–18). The viewable presence of glory is transferred from the fading experience of Moses to the face of Christ—the living resurrected Lord whose endless life embraces humanity into the glory of God (2 Cor 4:6).

> ¹⁴ *For the earth will be filled with the knowledge of the glory of the LORD, as the waters cover the sea.*
>
> Hab 2:14

> ²¹ *nevertheless—as I live, and as all the earth shall be filled with the glory of the LORD—*
>
> Num 14:21

What is the knowledge of the glory of the Lord? Habakkuk proposes a baptismal immersion of all creation into the life-giving Spirit of God; not a flood of destruction, or a return to chaos, but a flood of glory, an overwhelming embrace into the arms of God. Living temples of human beings all become one dynamic entity of life with all of its wonders.

Can it be that God will give of himself so completely that God and creation, God and humanity, become one? One reflection of the glory of God, without impediment or restraint?

A Prayer

Show me your glory, show me your ways, and show me your goodness, O Lord, for I know that I will be changed in any encounter with your holiness. You are creator and I am the creature that dances around your presence, ever longing for your word, your touch, your smile. Hide my soul in the cleft of a rock for I know that you will never lose me, you know me by name and I have found favor in thy sight.

Reading Twelve

Promises in Contrast

The Covenant Formula

⁷ I will give them a heart to know that I am the LORD;
and they shall be my people and I will be their God,
for they shall return to me with their whole heart
JER 24:7

The Wondering Psalm

³⁸ But now you have spurned and rejected him;
you are full of wrath against your anointed.
³⁹ You have renounced the covenant with your servant;
you have defiled his crown in the dust.
⁴⁰ You have broken through all his walls;
you have laid his strongholds in ruins.
⁴¹ All who pass by plunder him;
he has become the scorn of his neighbors.
⁴² You have exalted the right hand of his foes;
you have made all his enemies rejoice.
⁴³ Moreover, you have turned back the edge of his sword,
and you have not supported him in battle.
⁴⁴ You have removed the scepter from his hand,
and hurled his throne to the ground.

> [45] *You have cut short the days of his youth;*
> *you have covered him with shame.*
>
> Ps 89:38–45

Promises in Contrast

Covenant: this word, packed with religious baggage or overtones or meaning, is generally used to capture God in promises that are given absolute irrevocable status. Of course, God is a promise-making God who swears to make the articulated promise irrevocable. However, God (being God) can fulfill a promise after it has died. The God of Scripture is the Lord of resurrected life.

Abraham received promises and learned that God can keep his promises when death has already spoken. Sarah's menopause and Abraham's age cannot halt God's promises (and unlike us, God doesn't get in a hurry). Isaac's death would have only meant resurrection in the light of God's promise concerning this seed through whom the promises of Genesis 12:1–3 would be fulfilled. This is the interpretive position of the writer of Hebrews (Heb 11:17–19).

Nonetheless, ole Abe in his finiteness and limited life span seeks from God more than some promises: Abe seeks a covenant ceremony (Gen 15). God comforts Abraham with a ceremony that communicates God's faithfulness to his word. In effect, the ceremony reveals that God would be like a dismembered animal—that is, he would cease to be God—before abdicating the surety of his promises. From this story others would write that God cannot lie.

Collectively, the story reveals the wrestling of God and man: a faithful man up from the ground, a creature of the organic flotsam and jetsam of terra firma, and an all-powerful deity whose gentle hand reaches into the unfolding saga of human history to reveal God's self—slowly, surely, over time, knowing he will be misunderstood for a long, long time. God cannot be limited by time or death, and the man is confined to the limits of creation set in place by the God who is not bound. The faithful man meets the faithful God in a lived adventure of epic proportions, filled with drama, suspense, failure, loss, and even the cathartic power of tragedy.

The God is inviting the man upward, further from the ground, to walk in ways that fulfill the likeness and the image of the creating God. At the

Promises in Contrast

same time the man draws the infinite one into the world of the creature, "How am I to know?" asked Abraham. God's purposes cannot be stopped by humanity's limitations, but God works slowly, a thousand years bring no more change to the character, the holiness of God than any given day.

God has his word, the man has his ceremony; the one from above, the other from below. One is spirit and one is flesh. The tension is formed: the man has sought for more than the spirit of the word. But God acquiesces to the man's need; God is slow, patient, and works at his own pace.

> ... an all powerful deity whose gentle hand reaches into the unfolding saga of human history to reveal God's self, slowly, surely, overtime, knowing that he will be misunderstood for a long, long time.

God's revelation will require time and continue through the death of generations yet to come. The old man will have to accept his historical role as a person of faith and not see the fulfillment of the promises.

Although God swears in order to communicate that the word given is irrevocable, it seems that in relation to this other covenant into which Israel had put so much hope, the swearing part is the man's interpretation of God's will. That other notorious covenant of promise was given to a very different man than Abraham, an archetype in his own right; not a lowly man of faith, but a man of power, upheld by sword and the myth of royalty—that recipient of the covenant: David.

Interestingly, there is no swearing in the Davidic covenant proper in the book of Samuel (2 Sam 7). However, the Psalter claims that God swore to David; apparently to be God and to say "I will" is to swear (in the minds of Psalmists and assuming Nathan's word to David was complete). David shows no uncertainty and asks for no ceremony, but affirms God's promise with the confidence of a man accustomed to power and expects God to recognize the power of the state to stand in the place of God. In David's world, gods belong to land and peoples and cities; the universality of God-as-one is not yet fully conceived in Israel's populace, or in David.

So the Davidic covenant, that promise of a son of David perpetually upon the throne of David, fails. From the time of the Babylonian exile after the death of Zedekiah, Judah has no king upon a throne. The people of Israel cry out to God for the fulfillment of a promise to David. Their cry is that they should be a people (which to them means possessing land as a nation-state). God resurrects his dead promise and offers Israel a king unlike the murderous men who reign as kings and stand in the place of God over the people of God. Jesus—that "son of man" and "son of God"—is reluctantly a "son of David." This is not all that special considering the many children David sired through wives and concubines, and when you add to the mix Solomon's god-like procreating activities the descendants of David are numerous!

God's resurrected covenant looks nothing like the throne set up by David; it is a covenant in the heart, affirmed through faith. God has come down and mixed with the creature up from the ground. The fulfilling of the Davidic covenant translates into a new covenant, as affirmed by Jeremiah. The new covenant produces a people who belong to God inwardly; they will be his people and he their God. Israel will survive as a nation of people that belong to God, a people who are not constrained by borders, while awaiting the embrace of landedness. Their exile becomes a picture of how Christians are to live in the world, as aliens and strangers, people living in a city unseen, where justice and righteousness prevail. The divisive power of nationalism is lost to the universality of God's election of all peoples everywhere; all humanity is invited to the heavenly banquet. Jesus is not an archetype of faith in the likeness of, or in relation to, Abraham; Jesus is the last Adam, the preserving consummation of humanity into the being of God.

We the people of God desire to live in covenant, that is, with the same faithfulness as God. Yet it is our Lord Jesus who tells us not to swear, knowing that our promises can fail and we do not have the power to affirm our word in the world against the powers of death and chaos. We human beings have limitations and God does not. Vows are not covenants; they are sincere efforts dependent upon the grace of God to be lived out. A covenant is a legally binding promise. Not that any law can bind God; God freely binds God's self with his word, and affirms the yet unseen promise through the device of an oath and a ceremony offered for the sake of human beings. God's most powerful unilateral covenant of grace is seen in the crucifixion of Jesus whose own blood (life) is a guarantee of the new covenant imagined by Jeremiah.

Part of what it means to live out the image of God is to be a person that keeps their word to others, to live faithfully in relationship with others. Yet to bind oneself with an oath is not a Christian practice, for our Lord has clearly forbidden swearing as part of our practice.

> To image God is to be a person that keeps their word to others, to live faithfully in relationship with others.

We can vow to live a certain life of promise with the knowledge that human limitation, death, and chaos can inhibit our fulfillment of this promise. The freedom of choice and movement in the life of a human being is not to be co-opted by a covenant said to contain divine status or sanction. This same freedom also ensures God remains the Lord of life and can call people out of what they perceive to be an inviolable promise.

In the last sentence of the previous paragraph, I am not specifically addressing the marriage relationship; certainly God's desire is that the formation of married life and family be upheld as bulwarks against abuse in the name of freedom. God hates divorce (Mal 2:16); it is the obverse of his love to see marriage lived out through the vicissitudes of life's unpredictable changes and challenges. Marriage serves as a metaphor for our relationship with God as a people; it is the most challenging and sacred vow we can make between two human beings. All other vows fall short; they do not share in the natural binding powers of creation as marriage does.

There is no covenant relationship within the confines of an institution or movement or ecclesial community that is so binding as to restrict the freedom of its adherents from acting as agential beings whose first obedience is always to their Lord. This reality keeps the leader of any type of Christian ecclesial expression from obtaining the ultimate loyalty of those they are to serve. Such leaders must serve by example, not by a covenant become law.

Love that is ended by the violation of a spiritually perceived covenant between two persons is only human and has lost connection with the divine. The love of God is greater than the violation of a covenant. A broken covenant between human beings can relieve responsibilities formerly affirmed by the covenant. However, the love of God that fills our hearts is not dismissed in relation to, or for, either party.

We often sense the presence of this covenant concept when living together as the body of Christ in various ways. We know we have both spoken and unspoken obligations for one another, for the pursuit of serving and living as disciples of Jesus. This closeness—this longing for spiritual harmony, for uninterrupted relationship, for united purpose—is one of the signs of the Spirit; it is the presence of the covenant-keeping God. We must remember that God is the Lord over our perceptions of this covenant of spirit and the concept itself is not ultimately binding; God is not bound by our limits.

This wonderful reality of communal spiritual harmony—agreement in purpose and function—must ever remain open to the dissenting voice of every person's agential freedom. If it does not do so, it quickly empowers leaders to become keepers of law rather than ministers of spirit and grace. It is within the confines of power, of a subscribed plan, where dissent and questioning are not often welcome. And so grace and love fall victim to being sacrificed in the name of God.

Our struggle is not against flesh and blood, but against the exaltation of leadership, the absolutizing of method and dogma, the failure to love, to be empathetic, compassionate, and humble in the face of another human being. We are to exalt the least, remain open to the unpredictable wind of the Spirit, love self-sacrificially, even irrationally, and not concretize our perception of reality because so much is possible beyond our plans. God's work is larger than ours; God is not containable.

Most of all, we are to love, to reconcile, to be patient, to submit to the voice of God and recognize the freedom of each person to act in accordance with their faith. God's covenant does not exclude but invites all to come. Our covenants are limited to yes and no, to the agential freedom of the other and obedience to our one Lord.

> [33] "*Again, you have heard that it was said to those of ancient times, "You shall not swear falsely, but carry out the vows you have made to the Lord." [34] But I say to you, Do not swear at all, either by heaven, for it is the throne of God, [35] or by the earth, for it is his footstool, or by Jerusalem, for it is the city of the great King. [36] And do not swear by your head, for you cannot make one hair white or black. [37] Let your word be "Yes, Yes" or "No, No"; anything more than this comes from the evil one.*
>
> MATT 5:33–37

Reading Thirteen

Meaning and Suffering

Bleeding

Betrayed and abandoned on the road of life by those I loved most
An interrupted journey that refuses to return to normalcy
A scarred God walks with me and weeps at my side
Redemptive healing rides ahead on wings somewhere down the road
One day everything is gonna be alright
But today we bleed together, my God and I

Meaning and Suffering

Human suffering is inescapable; all of us will face some form of suffering, some tragedy before our life ends. The avoidance of suffering drives a large part of human life. We seek relief from suffering and secure our way in the world through all the efforts available to us. We secure shelter, clothing, food, water, and health care, while educating ourselves with skills that enable the enjoyment of life. This is not always an easy task because our efforts are disrupted by evil or chance.

Evil comes through the actions of other human beings in events like war, betrayal, greed, and slander. The evil of chance comes through events like disease and accidents, in floods, famines, earthquakes, and hurricanes. The most painful evil is related to the sphere of the human, whereas the evil of chance is found in the unpredictable forces of nature or human behavior. Evil and chance combined are a terribly lethal form of oppression and death.

Everyday Thoughts

> [11] *Again I saw that under the sun the race is not to the swift,*
> *nor the battle to the strong, nor bread to the wise,*
> *nor riches to the intelligent,*
> *nor favor to the skillful;*
> *but time and chance happen to them all.*
>
> Eccl 9:11

We have excelled in teaching about the presence of evil but have neglected the reality of chance.

Although rich with life, the world we live in is hostile to life. This dichotomy of hostility and richness is the tension that fills human experience. This truth is made dramatically evident in the birth of a child. Through great pain and the risk of life, a woman brings a child into the world. Likewise, a crop about to be reaped when a wind comes and destroys the plants is a mixture of the richness of life and of a world of hostility. The cycle of life and death appears to be an intrinsic necessity. Life, death, and suffering are linked together like an unbreakable chain. To be human is to die.

Death is also instructive when understood as a choice God made on our existence; we are not fit to live. God's word, like a flaming sword, has barred our way to the tree of life in the mythical garden. Jesus, however, showed us the way that leads to life eternal, the way of righteous suffering, the way of social change for rooting out evil, the way of faith that connects us to God our father, the way of grace where forgiveness offers a new beginning.

Jesus' death fulfills for us this reality. The priest of our confession—our model for imaging God—died. It is the death of Jesus that defines his life and humanity. It is the resurrection that defines God's purposes for human conformation in the image of God in Christ Jesus. Yet his death was filled with suffering brought on by the cruelty of hubris in high places of government, both civil and religious. In all this, Jesus rejected a violent response, and his words from the cross demonstrated love, humility, and hope-filled endurance.

> The cycle of life and death appears to be an intrinsic necessity. Life, death and suffering are linked together like an unbreakable chain. To be human is to die.

> [2] *looking to Jesus, the pioneer and perfecter of our faith, who for the sake of the joy that was set before him endured the cross, disregarding its shame, and has taken his seat at the right hand of the throne of God.*
>
> Heb 12:2

Meaning and Suffering

The hostility of the world in all its self-contained violence dehumanizes those who succumb to the way of the world (death and violence) as the way of humanity. Although it is human to die and death defines our reality, we are all wonderfully endowed with the reflection of our Creator, and as such, discover within ourselves a refusal to normalize death as an acceptable end for the life we have been given. We recognize time in its cycles of death and within our souls refuse to accept death as anything more than another hostile power that causes suffering. However, death permeates our world and our reality with such intrinsic presence that we blind ourselves to our participation at an existential level; death is inescapable.

> [11] *He has made everything appropriate to its time,*
> *and has put the timeless into their hearts,*
> *without men's ever discovering, from beginning to end,*
> *the work which God has done.*
>
> Eccl 3:11

Suffering is also caused by relationships that court death as an advantage; meaning, we use death as a power to exalt ourselves one against the other. This courting of death is nothing more than sin dressed up as self-interest. In the garden, Eve's self-interest challenged God's order for human behavior; God's voice that speaks with clarity is to be obeyed. All the structures of life flow from the gracious living God. Cain's self-interest (deification of self) resulted in the first murder and brought the human initiative of the city.

The myth of the individual has filled human cultures with structural evil in all our institutions. This is true even in the church. We have not pursued the inter-human purpose to function as one and instead have became a mass of individuals that can only be governed by force; that is, by violence, death's rotten fruit. The task of the church is to produce a "body" of believers that functions as one in Christ, the resurrected man. Likewise, those who believe are to live in accordance with an ethos that recognizes the oneness of humanity. This inter-human concept is clear in God's self-revelation: our sins affect our children (Exod 34:6–7), and not because God punishes them, but because sin is inter-human, sin is relational undoing, whether between God and a human, or between humans. Sin is never individual.

In this respect, the practice of spirituality is to fill the inter-human relations accomplished through institutions with righteousness and justice.

War is to be abhorred and the poor are to be lifted up through programs that fight poverty. In effect, spirituality without social change that opposes human suffering—especially as the result of human evil—is lacking the presence of the suffering God. Spirituality is not church-bound; it is lived within the social construct, in public, as light in the darkness.

Death reduces the meaning of life because it proposes a finality that humanity cannot overcome. Even if science could prolong human life indefinitely, we would still live with the pains of death found in hate, greed, excessive consumption, lust, anger, etc. We would still use violence to kill one another in a multiplicity of ways. This seems to be the teaching of the first chapters of Genesis prior to the flood: the human beings (those "sons of god," "fallen ones") that lived long lives had not become better persons but rather arrogant, self-interested individuals who sought to breed their seed into humanity through the abusive use of women as mere breeding chattel.

> War is to be abhorred, the poor are to be lifted up through programs that fight poverty, in effect spirituality without social change that opposes human suffering, human evil, is lacking the presence of the suffering God.

The contrapositive to self-interest (individualism) is to discover the meaning of life through faith. The object of faith is God; faith produces a God-centered self with interests greater than one's own life. Faith connects with the source of life in such a way as to overcome the sin that is in the world through death. The true individual is the one who walks in the way of Jesus—the one who speaks for justice and righteousness in resistance to all the powers of state and culture.

In the midst of pain, suffering, and death—in a world not the way it should be, where death wins—meaning is easily set aside for personal advantage (the individual's search for meaning). However, the healing of the self's need for meaning is found in eternity, in timeless memory, in the source of all life: the God who raises the dead. This faith in the resurrection empowers a human being to accept death with grace, to accept it in all its manifestations, and endure death with love, humility, and suffering. Suffering, after all, is inescapable. Even in the midst of suffering, a person can find that there is meaning to life; God is watching, and he cares deeply about how we live.

Suffering is the presence of death in the world and reaches deep into the human soul, particularly the suffering that is the direct result of abuse by another human being. Emotional suffering is debilitating in a way that damages the soul, and only the love of God can ultimately heal this type of suffering (trauma). This is so because God's healing allows a person to live with the suffering, while still loving the perpetrator. This kind of forgiveness—of power—we recognize as evidence of either spiritual depth or an enigma (rather than calling it divine).

> There is meaning to life because God cares deeply about how we live, because God is watching.

Is suffering meaningless? Does the suffering of the righteous have any advantage? Does suffering fulfill some purpose? First, the weight of suffering inflicted by one human being upon another cannot be blamed on God. This is because we are all learning to live, we have all sinned, and God is seeking to redeem all of us. The presence of evil is rooted in humanity's self-reliance and rejection of God.

We must learn to live, because we came into the world knowing nothing, the one task we must face on a daily basis is living in a way that brings meaning to life. God (life) and meaning are compatible; death and meaning are not. We give redeemed meaning to death through the manner in which we live and die. Since faith in God gives meaning to life, then the suffering of the righteous (any type of suffering) is our war against death. The only war a spiritual person should be involved in is a war against death, the enemy of God, an enemy that permeates human reality. We wage our war with faith, hope and love.

We are Stripped of Worldly Weapons and Rearmed with Spirit.

> *¹³ Therefore take up the whole armor of God, so that you may be able to withstand on that evil day, and having done everything, to stand firm. ¹⁴ Stand therefore, and fasten the belt of truth around your waist, and put on the breastplate of righteousness. ¹⁵ As shoes for your feet put on whatever will make you ready to proclaim the gospel of peace. ¹⁶ With all of these, take the shield of faith, with which you will be able to quench all the flaming arrows of the evil one. ¹⁷ Take the helmet of salvation, and the sword of the Spirit, which is the word of God.*
>
> EPH 6:13–17

There is suffering that is so horrid, so terrible, that the thought of it serving any good purpose, or any purpose at all, is inconceivable. The guilt of the perpetrator seems irredeemable and the pain of the victim beyond healing. However, God can heal the victim, and this must take place even if it is in the resurrection. Yet, even if the victim experiences healing, there is something left undone when the perpetrator is not brought to justice. I am not thinking of the punitive justice of human invention, but the justice of God, the merciful one. In the inter-human relationship the repentance of the perpetrator is essential for the healing of the perpetrator. However, the perpetrator's repentance must be accomplished before God and the victim. The perpetrator needs the forgiveness of the victim, whereas the victim can be healed by God. This is so because a truly repentant perpetrator feels the pain they have caused another and will seek to correct their actions. This is evidenced in the life of Paul. He cannot restore the lives he took, so he is moved to live with his conscience driven by an awareness of the grace he received; he remembers his victims. They are not alive for him to be reconciled to them, so he honors their deaths with his own life.

> [9] *For I am the least of the apostles, unfit to be called an apostle, because I persecuted the church of God.* [10] *But by the grace of God I am what I am, and his grace toward me has not been in vain. On the contrary, I worked harder than any of them—though it was not I, but the grace of God that is with me.*
>
> 1 COR 15:9–10

There is a qualitative difference between a victim and a perpetrator. God is portrayed throughout Scripture as hearing the cries of the afflicted—those who are victims of violence. An exception would be the interim period during the judgment of nations, e.g. abandonment of Israel to the powers of the Assyrian and Babylonian empires. In both cases, these two empires would later be judged for their treatment of Israel. Israel was guilty of intolerable violence prior to their destruction; and during their destruction, God did not heed their cries.

> There is meaning to life because God cares deeply about how we live, because God is watching. This does not alleviate the reality of suffering and I am convinced that suffering and death prepare us for absolute dependency upon God throughout the ages.

God's wrath is actually God's absence, allowing a violent empire to act cruelly towards an unprotected Israel.

The difference between a perpetrator and a victim is power.

Perhaps we all have the thought that pain did not need to be so intense, that some suffering is beyond reason, or possibility, for serving any good purpose. Our God is guilty of being merciful, and his culpability is taken up on a cross from which he cried, "Father forgive them for they know not what they are doing."

There is meaning to life because God cares deeply about how we live, because God is watching. This does not alleviate the reality of suffering and I am convinced that suffering and death prepare us for absolute dependency upon God throughout the ages.

Reading Fourteen

The Apocalypse: A Genre for Human Madness

The books of the Bible are written in a variety of genres that appeal to aspects of human need, personality, and phenomenon. Wisdom literature is my favorite because of the books of Ecclesiastes and Job (although Job defies a simple singular classification). Reading the narrative history of Israel and her patriarchs is enjoyable and subject to multiple meanings. The apocalyptic is subject to psychological analysis because it is the voice of prophetic trauma under the oppressive power of empire.

Apocalyptic Born

The apocalyptic genre of literature is an effort to communicate the insanity of hubris. The crimes of empire upon the excluded masses are the catalyst for producing apocalyptic feelings, and written visions. The writer's psychic placement is from the human experience of trauma. It has the quality of subversive literature in the sense that its critique is hidden from the object of its motivation (empire) because its application is universal. It leaves people subjected to the cruelty of empire with the hope that God will intervene before humanity self-destructs.

The apocalyptic genre is indicative of evil eruptions of meaninglessness in the realm of the living. The fluidity of apocalyptic thought, its universal appeal and application, defy adherence to a definable hermeneutical method. The genre leaves the imagination free to interpret meaninglessness as a sign that God must intervene, because the fear that humanity will destroy herself is overwhelming from the perspective of the writer. However, the reader is left free to reject the either/or hope for divine intervention and respond to the message by rejecting the injustices of empire and seeking the kingdom of God.

The apocalypticism of the Bible is born from the experience of a believing community of oppressed people; this voice is communicated via the author. As a cry, it rises from the oppressed that live under the pressures of pain, poverty, war, and prejudice; it is the voice of a traumatized population. Unable to articulate the cause of their duress, they revert to symbols and sweeping portrayals of cataclysmic eruptions that prohibit life. The apocalyptic mindset struggles at the edge of human madness to hold onto hope in times of structured murder and genocide. Like the imprecatory Psalms, the Apocalypse pictures God as an equalizing judge of punitive force. It is the cry of the suffering human voice that claims the perpetrator cannot understand their pain, unless that same pain is inflicted upon them.

The phenomenal understanding of humanity's seemingly inevitable condition of madness under the consolidation of centralized power in a single person is the intellectual attractiveness of the Apocalypse. Likewise, the writer's vision on the growth of economic power to global proportions displays foresight of an inspirational nature.

Perhaps the tracking of humanity through markings on the head and hand is understandable in another fashion than we imagine on this side of history. The Hebrew people were commanded to keep the Torah placed as a sign between their eyes (on the forehead) and tied as a sign on their hand. This command was not meant literally; rather, it is a picture of how to view the world and form reality.

Through the eyes, pictures enter the mind and we form our view of life. With the hand we work our will in the world. Our thoughts and the work of our hands are to be submitted to the word of God. In effect, we are already marked upon our heads and our hands; how we choose to live marks our lives. John of the Apocalypse envisioned a time when the violence of empire would attempt to rule the entire earth through force and economics. He envisioned a time when humanity would fall prey to (*Pax Romana*) the end of history as an ideal governing power of force. John's understanding of humanity reflects the vision of a person who understands reality. Humanity is self-destructive.

The Apocalypse is not an either/or revelation. The question, "Will humanity destroy herself or will God intervene?" is not the meaning of the Apocalypse. Rather, it is a portrayal of the tension between hope and despair, between trauma and the flourishing of life. The ideologies for human governance are all failures. Human beings are not meant to rule over one another. We are people building a city where the trying of our faith is more precious than gold. Our city's entrance is a pearl gate, concealing the earthiness within. God has joined humanity and the city of God is the people of God—the bride of Christ. This is not a literal city but a living temple of saints. The city is clear as glass; nothing is hidden.

There is the possibility that humanity will destroy herself in a nuclear or biological act of war. There is the possibility that the abuse of the earth's resources will result in an end to the present hubris of humanity. God can start over; God is not in a hurry. We need not learn a lesson of self-destruction if we will hear God's call to nonviolence, to love of neighbor, and love of God.

Contemporary Apocalyptic Fervor

Apocalyptic fervor is madness; it is the surrender to cosmic catastrophe as the inevitable course of life under the sun. The apocalyptic genre is unlike the other genres of literature in the Bible. Its appeal is to the insanity in all of us. For this reason, it attracts unstable minds. Apocalyptic literature is particularly attractive to weak-minded religious souls seeking to activate the coming of God by promoting apocalyptic feelings.

Apocalyptic teachers will always have an audience. Some people prefer delusion to intellectual tenacity and problem-solving. Apocalyptic end-time literature is also a distraction; it allows the religious person to ignore more important sociological issues and the spirituality of character development. For this reason, the marketing of "end-time" literature in affluent nations is common. This type of literature is not true to the heart and intent of the biblical genre.

However, the intent of apocalyptic literature of the Bible is not to provoke fear; its purpose is to relieve tension and challenge the alleged permanence of empire. The sign of prolific apocalyptic use in a society is indicative of the sure end to empire's hubris. It can also be an errant religious distraction. This is particularly so for people who delight in reducing intellectual effort to conspiracy theories. These fanatical readings, made with random numerical and picturesque connections, attempt to identify current events with apocalyptic passages. These alleged prophetic literal interpretations are misleading. Such was the practice of Hal Lindsey's *Late Great Planet Earth* and more recent literature like *The Harbinger*. The Y2K scandal has passed

The Apocalypse: A Genre for Human Madness

and the written works of profiteering writers disappeared, to be forgotten. The farce known as the Bible Code will return to entice another generation in due course. This is so because people prefer fantasy to the hard work of developing a life of mature spirituality and holistic biblical literacy—a life pursuing the will of God on earth for justice and righteousness.

It is frightful that people can be so emotionally enamored with end-time literature and not recognize the entire enterprise as a fruitless distraction. The biblical books that are identified as apocalyptic literature can also serve to gather in the power of insanity and bind it up in a genre that places the redemption of reality alongside the insanity of empire's hubris. Empires will fail and be judged, the world will continue; the redemptive work of God is both now and yet to come.

When rearing my children in the church I would tell them, "Live as though Christ will return at any moment, but plan your life as though Christ will not return in your lifetime." As I age I think I would add, "or for thousands of years." Apocalyptic literature provokes the question, "Will God let humanity destroy the world as we know it?" This is our fear

> The immorality and madness present in the overt amassing of nuclear weaponry is indicative of a society without God.

and it has never been as legitimately possible as it is in the present age. Knowing this, what manner of people ought we to be? The pursuit of God is not the pursuit of the end times; it is pursuing *shalom* for all humanity. It is to challenge the hubris of humanity in all of its manifestations and speak for the suffering masses, for the continuance of life under the sun.

Identification with the beast is consistent throughout history with the tyranny of empire. We are all marked: we are either beasts or children of God, either our hands work the will of God by serving the good and our mind by filtering reality through faith in God, or our hands bring destruction and our thoughts contribute to the encompassing power of empire.

The empires of this world all tend toward the hubris of standing in the place of God and seeking to govern the nations. However, the results are the development of empire's power to garner the resources of the earth at the expense of the nations. So, God accomplishes the cyclic maintenance of the kingdoms of the world through the rise and fall of empires. Empire's reach has developed a system of economics that governs the world; it is inevitable that this also must fail. The collapse of the economic system that supports empire can be restructured to enable the flourishing of other nations in a more just manner.

The need for biblical theologians that can address the complexities of ethics in a scientifically oriented world of technological possibilities that touch every part of our lives is immediate. An ignorant clergy reduces Christianity to irrelevance for addressing the issues faced in a world of instant information and runaway hubris. Jesus is the Lord who was, is, and is to come. He is the Lord of the past, the present, and of time yet to unfold with all of its complexity and surprises. The most pressing issue faced by the church is the development of mature believers that can be exemplars of spiritual living in a world needing to learn what it means to be human.

Reading Fifteen

Redemption: The End of History

Job 19:21–27 — My Translation

Be gracious to me, be gracious to me, you my friends.
For the hand of God has reached within me.
Why do you pursue me as God,
and from my flesh you are not satisfied?
Who will give—then—that my words were written?
Who will give—their inscription in a book?
With a chisel of iron, and filling with lead,
their engraving, in a rock, forever.
For I know that my redeemer is living
and at last upon the dust he will rise.
And after my skin, this skin which they have struck off,
Then from my flesh I shall see God.
Whom I shall see on my side.
And my eyes they will see, and not a stranger.
They cease, my emotions, within my bosom.

Redemption: The End of History

²⁵ᵇ *The suffering voice of humanity cried out from the inner reaches of his soul with a conviction held so deeply that his words became as well known as the sayings of the savior; "I know that my redeemer lives."*

JOB 19:25B

I know that my redeemer lives and he will undo all the ugliness of life with his wisdom and grace, and guide us into eternity. I know that redemptive activity is spiritual activity, that the gospel is redemptive, that redemption makes sense out of life. Redemption gives value to that which was lost; it finds the good in the midst of the mess. Loss surrenders to the grace of God.

Every human being is capable of surrendering to their moral conscience and in turn seeking to understand the relationship of the creator to the absence of justice. Needing to make sense out of life, human beings seek a theodicy that reconciles the concept of a moral or good God with an immoral or corrupt creation.

Redemption is a word that expresses a reality—a reality that seeks release and rises up from the human soul like a beacon to reveal the nature of God. Redemption is an expression of the sacred; it belongs to the concept of God's holiness. Redemption makes sense out of life, for it declares the value God places on each one of us in the midst of our suffering and sin.

Redemption in the present age is like a wind whispering through a crevice in the bedrock of a cave, where humanity lives in darkness, in violence, lost in desire like a beast to be restrained. The wind speaks of another world, another place, a place where the wind blows freely.

Redemption is a transformative power that enters into the spasms of history through earth-bound saints, whose lives reject the present state of affairs as intolerable. Redemption is a corrective, driven by love and grace. Redemption's correction rests on the other side of judgment, free from the restraints of vengeance or punishment.

> Redemption is a transformative power that enters into the spasms of history through earth bound saints whose lives reject the present state of affairs as intolerable.

In the end, redemption will chase history back to the beginning, undoing the hurt, destroying the evil, restoring and reconciling with the creative force of "In the beginning God created . . ." to discover the "last Adam" waiting with arms outstretched to embrace humanity into the fullness of his being, his Spirit, his existence.

To wholly participate in the redemptive activity of God is accomplished by souls freed from violence and liberated to love like Christ Jesus. There is no violence in God's redemptive activity, only suffering, as God gives God's self, God's love, into the hands of his beloved humanity.

Redemption in the world is accomplished through suffering the sins of others with love and grace, while ministering the love and Spirit of Jesus to the world by humbly resisting injustice with kindness. Where redemption is practiced, God is present. Where redemption is understood, people willingly give their lives for the healing of the world. When redemption is received, people meet God—Christ in us, the hope of God that we might know and walk in his ways.

I know that my redeemer lives and that in my flesh I will see God.

Reading Sixteen

A Psychology of Illness in Psalm 38

Understanding the Sick

It is my purpose in this essay to align sections of Psalm 38 with the mental movements of human beings who suffer debilitating illness or injury. Through this process, I will demonstrate how the Psalm reveals a pattern for ministering to persons that are struggling with the loss of their health. I will discuss six stages expressive of the mental movements of a human being suffering illness or injury. Psalm 38 provides a pattern for responding with wisdom, good counsel, hope, and comfort to a person suffering illness or injury.

A Psychology of Illness in Psalm 38

First: Consciousness of Sin

¹ O LORD, do not rebuke me in your anger,
or discipline me in your wrath.
² For your arrows have sunk into me,
and your hand has come down on me.
³ There is no soundness in my flesh because of your indignation;
there is no health in my bones because of my sin.

Initially the sufferer acknowledges their sin and relates feelings of guilt as cause for their condition. This seems to be a normal response by those who suffer debilitating illness or injury; they think God is angry with them for some past sin. In their mind and heart they seek some understanding for what is often the arbitrariness of calamity in the form of illness. This first mental movement of the ill is to be countered by the assurance that they are not suffering as punishment for sin.

Second: Loss of Strength Sufficient for Living

⁵ My wounds grow foul and fester because of my foolishness;
⁶ I am utterly bowed down and prostrate;
all day long I go around mourning.
⁷ For my loins are filled with burning,
and there is no soundness in my flesh.
⁸ I am utterly spent and crushed;
I groan because of the tumult of my heart.
⁹ O Lord, all my longing is known to you;
my sighing is not hidden from you.
¹⁰ My heart throbs, my strength fails me;
as for the light of my eyes—it also has gone from me.

The crippling power of illness can completely halt and inhibit the interaction of a human being in the affairs of life. Loss of mobility, coupled with pain, leaves a person incapable of relational involvement, incapable of fulfilling the activity required to participate in the joys of daily life. Hopes and dreams vanish in the despair of pain and immobility.

The second mental movement of the ill is to be countered by hope. Hope is brought about through prayer. Hope is brought with stories of other human beings who recovered from a similar condition.

Third: Isolation from Humanity

¹¹ My friends and companions stand aloof from my affliction,
and my neighbors stand far off.

Human beings fear the chaotic powers that disrupt a flourishing life with pain and suffering. The fear is so deeply rooted in the psyche that many prefer to leave the suffering person alone, treating them as they would someone that had died. This irrational fear is also accompanied by a sense of feeling inadequate or incapable of helping a person in their pain.

The third mental movement of the suffering person can be overcome by touch. Isolation melts at the touch of a caring friend or minister. Touch violates the stigma of being "untouchable" or "unclean," and brings a needed connection with the living.

Fourth: Paranoia over the Thoughts and Intents of People

[12] Those who seek my life lay their snares;
those who seek to hurt me speak of ruin,
and meditate treachery all day long.

A suffering human being imagines the relief or gain that some will experience if the sufferer were to cease to exist. As a result, a state of paranoia about the thoughts of others can engulf the suffering individual.

The fourth mental movement of a suffering person can be overcome by love: valuing their life and telling them how their absence will be felt if they are gone.

Fifth: Loss of Voice or Influence among the Living

[13] But I am like the deaf, I do not hear;
like the mute, who cannot speak.
[14] Truly, I am like one who does not hear,
and in whose mouth is no retort.

The loss of voice in the Bible is indicative of suffering the power of murder. In the Cain and Abel story the first victim of the first murder never speaks. Jesus' murder becomes so evident that he does not speak to defend himself before his accusers. Human beings seek to be contemporary with others, but when they are removed from life they lose the ongoing dialogue of community. Of course, there are universal realities we can always converse about and these are most important in the scope of life and death.

The fifth mental movement of a suffering human being is countered by listening. A suffering isolated human being needs a voice, needs to speak, and needs to be heard. It is this process that can enable the suffering person to come to the place that they can move to the final stage of their mental movements.

Sixth: Recognition of God as the Only Source of Comfort

The psalm closes in a prayer of faith that relies solely upon God to be the answer for their need. The suffering soul counters the voices of those that sought to profit from their death by confessing complete dependency upon God for life. The prayer of repentance at this point is genuine and not a response to their illness. The heart of the suffering person is cleansed through their prayer, and their peace is established through hope in God.

The sixth and final mental movement of the suffering person is accompanied with smiles and confirming speech and prayers.

> [15] *But it is for you, O LORD that I wait; it is you,*
> *O Lord my God, who will answer.*
> [16] *For I pray, "Only do not let them rejoice over me,*
> *those who boast against me when my foot slips."*
> [17] *For I am ready to fall, and my pain is ever with me.*
> [18] *I confess my iniquity; I am sorry for my sin.*
> [19] *Those who are my foes without cause are mighty,*
> *and many are those who hate me wrongfully.*
> [20] *Those who render me evil for good are my adversaries because I follow after good.*
> [21] *Do not forsake me, O LORD; O my God, do not be far from me;*
> [22] *make haste to help me, O Lord, my salvation.*

Reading Seventeen

The Struggles of Reading and Writing Theology

Trembling

I fear myself
My flesh bleeds into my words
Spontaneity replaced with choice
The moment stretches into brooding over words
Writing is not speaking
It lives beyond me

Reading the Bible as Scripture

People claim with deep conviction their belief in the Scripture as God's word. And for them it is, inasmuch as they are allowed to pick and choose pieces that serve their purposes. However, instead of facing the Scripture in all its antiquity, in all its foreignness, in all its crude record of murder, war, and genocide—often accomplished in the name of God—these confessors of Scripture practice ignoring, prefer ignorance, rather than facing or wrestling with how this strange book is to be read.

Answers to complex pieces of Scripture do not come easy, and attempting to defend some passages to preserve the book's integrity at the cost of letting its claims about God, or human behavior, off easy is religious chicanery. This book, this word of God to us, is mere ink on pages; but to ascribe meaning to the collected works lifts the ink from the pages to dwell in the minds of human beings. Are we to pick and choose, to cut and dice?

Are we to reduce to aphorisms this magnum opus of literary genius from ages past?

How am I—how are we—to read legislation that is deemed to be Torah, holy, instructive, when that legislation appears to sanction genocidal acts in the name of God? If I claim we are to have the intelligence to read it as a record of failure, to claim it is a record of errant religious faith, would I not be ostracized from the faith? Who am I to question God's word? Or, perhaps I use my imagination and with great effort and dialectical skill expose the meaning of these passages to be other than what they appear on the surface; will I be a man of wisdom? Why must I wrestle with these inconceivably dark passages of Scripture? Is it because it's only in the wrestling, only in the questioning—the refusal to accept them at face value—that I meet God?

> Are we to reduce this magnum opus of literary genius from ages past to aphorisms?

Is not my drive and concern expressive of my belief that this book is to be read as God's word—not in a literal way, but in a way that draws me closer to God, closer to illuminating the darkness? Does knowing God expose that which is not truly descriptive of him? The truth is, I must take God with me when reading this word of God, this holy book. When he accompanies me in this venture, together we critique its claims and expose the writers as mere humans. I, the reader, judge the original author's words, giving meaning to these words, and perhaps even meaning the writer never expected. I arrive at the text in all my weakness, with faith, with God in tow and moving ahead of me. When I arrive at the text, I bring my revelation of God with me and attempt to reconcile God and text. He teases me with thoughts and enlightens my mind to read, oh but to put it on paper, I know not how. To speak it, to teach it, to live in the moment and enjoy God flowing through my mind and words, releasing from my lips with speed and preciseness—such delight.

Writing lacks the living voice, the encounter, the moment, the totality of the communicator in flesh. Writing is an impossible task, an art, a challenge. I will always be more than the words I write, and God is always more than the word we read.

Reading Nineteen

Theological Musings

Learning to think theologically is both a discipline to be practiced through rigorous study and an exercise in spiritual sentience. Briefly, I will suggest some basic guidelines for reading the Bible theologically. First, in order to find God in the text, look for mercy. Second, be aware that you bring yourself to the text. With this in mind, it is imperative that disciplined study and openness to hearing from God are combined efforts. The theological effort is to hear the text speak as God's word to us.

Instructive Passages for Theological Growth

First Musing—Genesis 4:23–24

A Poem from a Suspicious Character

What are we to do with this poetic speech from the mouth of Lamech? Consider that the first polygamist in the Genesis record is Lamech. The names of Lamech's wives are taken from Hebrew words meaning "ornament" and "shadow." Adah is an ornament; she is the beautiful wife. Zillah is left to live in the shadow of Adah. Lamech's killing of a young man for some menial assault is used to hold his wives in an unnatural relationship. His poem is a subtle threat to his wives and a pronouncement of power with God. Lamech suggests that taking a life in an act of vengeance for a small matter is an act that God will bless with protection, just as he did for Cain. Lamech's theology is void of mercy and seeks self-preservation on religious grounds. The religious, or theological, element drawn into the poem by Lamech's claim of protection suggests that Lamech has power to take the lives of his wives if they offend him. Lamech's story portrays how religion is misused to support violence, while denying responsibility for such violence.

> [23] Lamech said to his wives: "Adah and Zillah, hear my voice; you wives of Lamech, listen to what I say I have killed a man for wounding me, a young man for striking me. [24] If Cain is avenged sevenfold, truly Lamech seventy-sevenfold."
>
> GEN 4:23–24

The poem is written to subject the women to the command of Lamech ("Hear my voice . . . listen to what I say"). They have meaning (names) only as possessions ("his wives . . . wives of Lamech"). The purpose for bragging about his murder is to threaten his wives with violence if they do not please him. The final line establishes a culture of religious-based violence.

The theological lessons from Lamech's poem are placed in contrast to the earlier lessons of Genesis. First, God created a male and a female to begin and perpetuate the human family. Second, God's act of mercy to forgive Cain was not an approval for killing or a pattern of protection to be established for offenders.

Theological Lesson Based Upon Lamech's Poem:

Polygamy is an act of violence against women, and is justified by the misuse of religious belief.

Second Musing—Genesis 6:1–7

Eugenics and the End of Humanity

The beauty of women and the desire of men to "take" more than one wife have already been explored in the poem of Lamech. Lamech can multiply his descendants through his multiple wives. Genesis 6:1–7 is a brief story that sets up the reason for the cataclysmic return of the waters of chaos that swallow the earth and mark another beginning—a re-start—in the Genesis narrative.

> [1] When people began to multiply on the face of the ground, and daughters were born to them, [2] the sons of God saw that they were

> *fair; and they took wives for themselves of all that they chose.* ³ *Then the LORD said, "My spirit shall not abide in mortals forever, for they are flesh; their days shall be one hundred twenty years."* ⁴ *The Nephilim were on the earth in those days—and also afterward—when the sons of God went in to the daughters of humans, who bore children to them. These were the heroes that were of old, warriors of renown.* ⁵ *The LORD saw that the wickedness of humankind was great in the earth, and that every inclination of the thoughts of their hearts was only evil continually.* ⁶ *And the LORD was sorry that he had made humankind on the earth, and it grieved him to his heart.* ⁷ *So the LORD said, "I will blot out from the earth the human beings I have created—people together with animals and creeping things and birds of the air, for I am sorry that I have made them."*
>
> GEN 6:1–7

The word "Nephilim" is better translated as "the fallen ones." Nephilim is parallel or synonymous with the "sons of God." Within the flow of the early chapters of Genesis, there are men of advanced years living in the midst of a large, youthful population. In an effort to preserve the purity of their seed and secure some sense of life after death, they take multiple wives for the purpose of bearing many children. The eugenic practices of these men mark an end to the ordained family structure established in the garden. Further, the abuse of women is coupled with this action. The violence against familial structure and women is the catalyst that propels humanity into a state of corruption and evil.

Theological Lesson from Genesis 6:1–7

Eugenics, or the breeding of humanity, is a self-destructive act that God will not tolerate, the underlying structures of reality that form creation will erupt against such activity. Human flourishing belongs to God, and human procreation is not to be manipulated by societal powers of wealth, science, or government.

Third Musing—Hosea 4:11–14

> ¹¹ *Wine and new wine take away the understanding.* ¹² *My people consult a piece of wood, and their divining rod gives them oracles.*

Theological Musings

> *For a spirit of whoredom has led them astray, and they have played the whore, forsaking their God.* [13] *They sacrifice on the tops of the mountains, and make offerings upon the hills, under oak, poplar, and terebinth, because their shade is good. Therefore your daughters play the whore, and your daughters-in-law commit adultery.* [14] *I will not punish your daughters when they play the whore, nor your daughters-in-law when they commit adultery; for the men themselves go aside with whores, and sacrifice with temple prostitutes; thus a people without understanding comes to ruin.*
>
> Hos 4:11–14

The piece of Scripture above is contained within an inclusio that forms a proverb. Verses 11 and 14e form the proverb. *Wine and new wine take away understanding, thus a people without understanding comes to ruin.*

The inclusio sets apart this piece as constituting a theological lesson to be learned, studied, and heeded. I will begin with some comments and proceed to form a theological lesson or statement. Israel's whoredom is the abandonment of the living God for the alluring temptations of wine, merriment, superstition, and fertility worship. The orgies on the mountains were for igniting the spirit of fertility to bless the land with growth and life. The practice of temple prostitutes was maintained to justify the maintenance of brothels for wealthy men.

Hosea points out that the older fathers (possibly grandfathers) cannot ensure that their daughters and daughters-in-law are procreating for the growth of the family. This group of older men is held responsible for the decline of Israel's religious and sexual purity. However, the most remarkable statement is that God will not punish the women for their sin. The men are held accountable for the sexuality of the women.

The proverb makes the claim that the people have lost understanding. First, their understanding is lost due to the consumption of wine. Second, however, is that the last half of the proverb is connected to verse 14, which reveals the ideology that Israel does not understand. Israel does not understand that men determine the sexual mores of a society (or they simply blame and victimize the women). The males of Israel were circumcised as a sign of their oath to the covenant that Yahweh would be their God and they would be his people—that their sexuality belonged to God because their seed belonged to God.

Everyday Thoughts

Perhaps men are more capable of abstaining from sex than women. This passage explicitly suggests that males are responsible for the sexual behavior of women. The women act promiscuously because the men formed social structures that require their sexual compliance.

Theological Lesson

Males are responsible for the sexual behavior of women in society, and God does not hold women culpable for their sexual failings when men have structured society in a way that exploits them and their sexuality.

Reading Nineteen

God's Word, Archaic Laws, and Torah as Teaching

Biblical law ceases to function as word, as spirit, when it is absolutized. The Torah is first and foremost instructive; it is to be applied with mercy and grace. The law was written to regulate human behavior because God could not stop people from living immorally or unethically. The laws of the Torah seek to communicate the human condition in contrast to the holiness of God.

Think for Yourself

Since Christians view the entire corpus of the Old Testament as God's word, it is imperative that we learn how to appropriate the teaching of the Torah's archaic laws into our theology. I believe these laws can speak beyond their setting in time because of my experience in reading and interpreting them within the confines of applied theological wisdom. Towards the end of this article, I will offer some applicable readings of some odd and distant laws contained in Deuteronomy. First, I will place the laws within their cultural, historical, and literary setting.

The book of Deuteronomy begins with the need for Moses to direct the nomadic peoples of Israel with legislative regulations in order to resolve conflicts and bring order to their growing social dynamics. After the wilderness period, a generation has aged into the majority populace of the people of Israel and do not have memories of Egyptian bondage. The aging Moses is preparing to die and must connect his people with their past, while preparing them for a future he will not experience.

> ² *he said to them: "I am now one hundred twenty years old. I am no longer able to get about, and the LORD has told me, 'You shall not cross over this Jordan.'*
>
> DEUT. 31:2

The defining relational and revelatory event for Israel was the theophany at Sinai (Horeb). It is arguable that the defining relational event with Israel, from God's perspective, was when the slaves followed him into the wilderness (Jer 2:1–3). Sinai does not happen without the slaves' willingness to follow the invisible God, who has won their liberation from Egyptian injustice. This generation with Moses on the plains of Moab must be connected with their history in a way that makes them accountable to the revelation of God at Sinai. Moses represents the past; the life of Israel's people is to change from nomadic to landed persons. Prior to entering the land, Moses will create an event that replaces the present with the memories of the past. Moses will define this people as God's covenant people.

> Moses will speak to the generation entering the land as though they had experienced the Sinai event.

> ² *The LORD our God made a covenant with us at Horeb.* ³ *Not with our ancestors did the LORD make this covenant, but with us, who are all of us here alive today.*
>
> DEUT. 5:2–3

The people of Israel have been cleansed of their warrior class—those who sought to fight (Deut 2:16). They must learn to follow the Lord into the land as dependent upon God for the land as gift, as their fathers had been dependent upon God for deliverance from Egyptian power and enslavement. However, their failure to trust God for divine aid comparable to the events in Egypt is already brought into question, and Moses blames the people for his exclusion from entering the Promised Land.

> ³⁷ *Even with me the LORD was angry on your account, saying, "You also shall not enter there".*
>
> DEUT. 1:37

The Lord's disappointment with Moses seems to be directly related to the spying episode. Moses' complicity in the event leads the people to

God's Word, Archaic Laws, and Torah as Teaching

suppose that their own efforts at cunning and warring will be necessary to take the land. In contrast, Moses instructs them with a reminder of God's leading from Egypt to the present. The error is revealed when the men strap on battle gear and seek to fight to take the land. Their actions sit in opposition to Moses' words. I suggest that even Moses has some reservations about the ability of both God and man to avoid war, when forming nations come into contact. This is so simply because God would need to intervene with acts of power inconsistent with his purposes in the story of redemption.

> [30] The LORD your God, who goes before you, is the one who will fight for you, just as he did for you in Egypt before your very eyes, [31] and in the wilderness, where you saw how the LORD your God carried you, just as one carries a child, all the way that you traveled until you reached this place.
>
> Deut 1:30–31

The beginning of Deuteronomy is rich with the growing tension between God and Israel. The temptation to war is greater than the faith of the people to trust God to deliver to them the land. God's efforts to produce a non-warring people are failing. Israel began their war with God when they rejected his voice at Sinai (Deut 5:30). Unwilling to take the risk of peace and exercise trust in God, Israel will adopt violent, unrestrained force to take the land. It is the rejection of hearing and obeying that results in the necessity of the commandment, the statutes, and the ordinances (Deut 6:1). As Moses delivers his series of speeches in Deuteronomy, he presents the challenge of hearing and obeying, over and against the temptation to self-attainment via taking the land by force. Faith and violence sit in opposition to one another throughout the conquest of the land.

> Faith and violence sit in opposition to one another throughout the conquest of the land.

The commandments—the statutes and ordinances—are to be understood as attempts to regulate Israel's failure to live in harmony with the voice (the presence) of God. The faith that God admired in the people when they first left Egypt is not found alive in the people who are about to enter the land. Jeremiah will refer to this moment when Israel left Egypt as a covenantal agreement on Israel's part, which meant that hearing and obeying was evidenced by following God, even when it seemed unreasonable according to natural realities (Jer 11:1–8). They have not followed because they rejected God's voice, an action that set them in a place of opposition to God. They are at war with God in their hearts and in the world. As a result, they practice violence and become their own deliverers. The God of peace and the gods of war are incompatible.

War is an immoral practice and morality cannot be legislated, but only governed through regulations that seek to limit the damages of immorality. The good king Josiah was reared from an early age by scribes that helped him become a king praised by the chronicler (2 Chr 34:1,2). However, Josiah's reform was a failure, and the prophet Jeremiah came on the scene to bring a message of exile. The failure of Josiah indicates that legislating morality according to religious beliefs cannot ensure change in the hearts of people. Josiah should have learned from the Torah that the law could only regulate behaviors in society; it merely limits damage done by immoral hearts. Hearts belong to God and God is a living voice that speaks through prophets, not through the king's forced legislation.

I think we now have a sufficient theological backdrop for reading the archaic laws contained in the book of Deuteronomy. I will reiterate my basic hermeneutical lens for reading the Torah and its archaic laws. First, the Torah as God's word is instructive for life. Study of the Torah brings wisdom and enables the one who listens to God's voice to derive theological truth from it. And second, the archaic regulations we will be reading and exploring are to be viewed as attempts to regulate wrongdoing. This means that immoral practices cannot be stopped by legislation, but they can be regulated to limit the damage done.

Statutes and Ordinances

I will begin by making a statement on the continually recurring deterrent: the death penalty. Israel's God is merciful by self-definition (Exod 34:6). The Torah statutes and ordinances are not like Israel's God. In the statutes and ordinances, the death penalty reaches far beyond the crime of murder; the execution of offenders is a communal activity. There is no record that Israel ever carried out the death penalty for these offenses. The constant refrain of the death penalty for various offenses in the Torah is instructive for understanding the seriousness of sin's power to bring death into the community. These laws are merely starting points from which to regulate behavior.

The book of Deuteronomy is rich with meaningful texts that offer authentic instruction as God's word, which can speak to our current social and political realities. For example, chapter fifteen is instructive for addressing the failings of capitalism's justification for the unending acquisition of wealth by a few. This chapter also validates the efforts of a good employer to care for his or her employees. Chapter seventeen requires the leaders of nation-states to refrain from warring, opulence, exaltation, and using their power to get women. Leaders are to be reminded daily of their responsibility to act morally before God.

Protecting Victims

Deuteronomy 21:10–14 is an interesting law governing the taking of women as captives after destroying the male population of a people. First, we begin by acknowledging that the law is written to govern immoral practices that Moses is powerless to stop. In this case, the immoral practices are war, slaughtering the male population, and the abuse of women.

> [10] When you go out to war against your enemies, and the LORD your God hands them over to you and you take them captive, [11] suppose you see among the captives a beautiful woman whom you desire and want to marry, [12] and so you bring her home to your house: she shall shave her head, pare her nails, [13] discard her captive's garb, and shall remain in your house a full month, mourning for her father and mother; after that you may go in to her and be her husband, and she shall be your wife.[14] But if you are not satisfied with her, you shall let her go free and not sell her for money. You must not treat her as a slave, since you have dishonored her.
>
> DEUT. 21:10–14

At the heart of the law is a guiding principle: the preservation of life. However, the law beyond the Ten Commandments must preserve life within the context of the failure of humanity to abide by the Decalogue. It is important to note that winning in war meant God was with you and losing meant God refrained from going with you. The prophets would utilize this same theology. Israel did not always win, and if they failed to obey the Lord, then they were subject to destruction. Yet the Lord was merciful and could not make a full end of Israel because of his love and promises.

In this statute, Moses seeks to reestablish some life-producing order to the undoing of the good by the practices of war and male dominance. After war, life must regain some civility, some sense of normalcy. Moses could not stop the men from taking women captive. The lives of these women had been preserved and their dignity had to be recovered, in spite of the horrors of war. Moses wrote this law to protect foreign women from ongoing abuse, and to assimilate them into this new cultural world. Conquering a people includes the conquering of the women through sexual dominance. Moses resisted this activity with his law. In spite of war and talk of enemies, men and women like each other. The Israelite male could marry captive women, or the women were to be set free (to marry someone else).

In this case, Moses assumes the captive woman was powerless in the decision to become a wife to the conquering soldier. Her beauty is the reason the man has taken her captive. Her world has been destroyed, her family and culture and people are destroyed. She needs time to grieve; she needs some symbolic signs in her own life that aid in her recovery. The male that has taken her needs to know her as a human being and not as a prize of war to be abused. So Moses commands that her head be shaved, her nails cut, and her clothing changed. The woman has lost her identity and it is expressed in the dramatic signs that diminish her beauty. The man's attraction to her must now be formed around her behavior in his home for the period of a month. A month hardly seems sufficient time, yet the man must decide to take her or not, before her hair can grow back and her attractiveness be decorated. If the male finds the woman disagreeable then she is to be set free. She is not a slave, her dignity is restored, and the man is guilty of dishonoring her if he chooses not to keep her. She is the victim, the one dishonored, and so she is set free. The captive woman is not entirely powerless: her ability to determine her status as captive or wife can be gained if she so desires, she just has to be disagreeable with her captor, or not.

> Conquering a people includes the conquering of the women through sexual dominance.

This reading teaches us that Moses' purpose for writing the law was to protect the victim. The law demonstrates Moses' acute awareness of human behavior and psychological needs. War is immoral; it produces victims, particularly women and children. The complete slaughter of the male population points to war as a predominantly male practice. Warring indicates the failure of men to live in harmony with the needs of women in general. Male dominance over women opposes the concept that women reflect the image of God in complete equality with males.

Midlife Crisis in the Male

Jesus affirms the interpretive reading of the law as a device to regulate immorality in his response to the Pharisees.

> *⁴ They said, "Moses allowed a man to write a certificate of dismissal and to divorce her." ⁵ But Jesus said to them, "Because of your hardness of heart he wrote this commandment for you.*
>
> Mark 10:4–5

With the concept that law's first obligation is to preserve life, and that the statutes and ordinances were written to limit damage done by infractions of the law, we will look at the reasoning behind Moses' divorce law.

> *¹ Suppose a man enters into marriage with a woman, but she does not please him because he finds something objectionable about her, and so he writes her a certificate of divorce, puts it in her hand, and sends her out of his house; she then leaves his house ² and goes off to become another man's wife. Then suppose the second man dislikes her, writes her a bill of divorce, puts it in her hand, and sends her out of his house (or the second man who married her dies); her first husband, who sent her away, is not permitted to take her again to be his wife after she has been defiled; for that would be abhorrent to the LORD, and you shall not bring guilt on the land that the LORD your God is giving you as a possession.*
>
> Deut. 24:1–4

Moses' law in this case is an effort to make a man think carefully about divorcing his wife. Men tend to seek younger, more attractive women, which can result in them divorcing the mother of their children. This midlife crisis in the male is a problem, and women are the victims. The victimization of the woman is particularly so in a male-dominated society, where the woman must remarry in order to survive. So Moses' law makes the man think carefully before divorcing his wife because Moses will not let him have her back. Young replacement wives cannot substitute for the enduring relationship of time, memory, and children.

This statute is interested in protecting the female victim from the immorality of the dominant male. It addresses the males and their midlife desire to preserve youth beyond time's limitations. The value of the woman is upheld throughout this statute. Although it is lacking in many of rights that women in our society have, it is likely the best Moses could do in his society. Once again, the need for male-female equality is evident and immorality is on the side of the male and the will of good (of God) on the side of the female.

Procreative Powers are Sacred

This is an interesting statute and its meaning is important for understanding sexuality, and even circumcision.

> [11] *If men get into a fight with one another, and the wife of one intervenes to rescue her husband from the grip of his opponent by reaching out and seizing his genitals,* [12] *you shall cut off her hand; show no pity.*
>
> DEUT 25:11–12

Let us begin by considering the problem, which Moses is attempting to address, and the instructive element of the statute. From time to time men argue and fight. Moses cannot stop men from fighting. Women intervene to save their husbands and this is to be expected. The problem in this scenario is that men did not wear pants and thus their genitals were easily accessed. It seems that Moses seeks to preserve the procreative powers of males (which are useless without the female). In Israel, circumcision is a covenantal seal between God and the male population. Males are required to be responsible for their procreative powers, controlling their sexuality and accepting the responsibility of producing children. The power to procreate is considered sacred and to damage a male in an effort to stop a fight is inexcusable; it is an effort to regulate and identify violence that prohibits the continuation of life. This same type of legislation is in laws that prohibit cutting fruit trees for siege works or salting the ground. Moses calls for the woman's hand to be cut off. I expect that the penalty is to be viewed as instructive deterrent and not absolute for practice. The penalty enhances the importance of the male procreative powers. Fights happen and a man's reproductive powers (blessing) should not be lost at the hands of an intervening female.

Theological Lesson

When we understand that these laws or statutes were written to regulate the damage done by uncontrolled immorality, then we can begin to unlock the reasons for the laws. Reading these archaic laws requires recognition that they are religious texts that are to be studied for their instructive value. The laws reflect wisdom and insight into human needs and behavior. Theological readings are required for many of the laws and we are prepared to read these laws when our theology has been properly framed by careful reading of the entire Torah.

Reading Twenty

Spiritual Intelligence

The ABCs

When teaching the maturation of the intellect in conjunction with spiritual maturation, a helpful pedagogic tool is the ABCs of spiritual intelligence. These are: awareness, burden, and culpability.

Sentience, Intellect, Spiritual Maturation, and Spiritual Intelligence

Spirituality is the integration of intellect, sentience, and faith; it is not one over the other, nor is it one and not the other. Spirituality begins with faith and produces the wisdom that finds God in the world. Wisdom is articulated in words and not reducible to intuitive claims without intellectual validation and affirmative observation in the world. Christian spirituality is relational and not method, nor is it free from responsibility to the Scripture.

Certainly it is true that sensitivity to the presence of God is a positive indicator of the process of spiritual development and maturation. However, fellowship with God is not mere euphoric peace that overwhelms in order to produce a serene personality unmoved by the events of the world. Although spiritually endowed cathartic moments of emotional healing result in feelings of euphoria, these experiences are not signs of maturation. The spiritual person that is growing in relationship with God in Christ is faced with intellectual catharsis—moments when the clarity of truth sits in contrast to the present.

It is a mistake to think that spirituality is purely sentient and bypasses the intellect. The intellect is where words are formed. Words provide definition for comprehending reality and are the medium through which God clarifies his acts of self-revelation. It is also a mistake to assign spirituality solely to the intellect; it is the integration of sentience and intellect that produces evidence of spiritual maturation.

I want to explore the integration of sentience and intellect as participants in the forming of the spiritual person. The sentient person of faith understands that God has created the world and thereby finds God speaking through creation, through the underlying structures of reality. The sentience that participates in the forming of the spiritual person begins with faith; that is, God exists as benevolent goodness and the world must be interpreted through this truth. This same truth must guide the intellect when reading Scripture or adding the sentient to the movements of the intellectual pursuit to articulate.

The sensing, feeling, intuitive reality (or sentience) that I am writing about is faith-based, relationally formed, and interdependent upon intellectual integration for mature manifestation. Likewise, the intellect that forms spiritual maturation is faith-based and integrated with sentience; sentience that is matured with understanding and not mere intuition.

Spiritual maturity lives comfortably with the concept of a just God and an unjust world. Spiritual intelligence is evidenced when God is found in the contradictions that form between the two. Knowing God in spirit and truth is the integration of sentience and intellect, it is the combination of mystic and theologian in a single person.

The apostle James will proclaim that God gives wisdom freely to all who desire. Proverbs 8 portrays wisdom as speaking clearly from multiple locations so that all might hear. Paul locates all wisdom in the revelation of God found in Christ upon the cross. This is the starting point for the Christian. The great question is: what does it mean to have a crucified God? Paul does not reduce the message of the cross to simplistic explanations, but to a great mystery that the wise of the world cannot grasp. Paul will insist that the mystery of this wisdom is available to the mature. Paul seeks to develop spiritual maturation among the Corinthians and uses words to articulate this once hidden wisdom. Paul clearly views the revelation of God's self-sacrifice to be at the center of all wisdom and simplistic explanations lack comprehension of the fullness of the depth of wisdom contained in the cross.

At this point I want to establish the concept of spiritual intelligence. I stated earlier that, spiritual intelligence is evidenced when God is found in the contradictions that form between the two, that is, a just God and an unjust world. Spiritual intelligence is not providing an answer for all situations and contradictions that form between our understanding of God and our experience of reality; rather it is a way of interpreting the world for living a spiritual life.

Spiritual intelligence (like spiritual sentience and intellect) begins with the concept that God is good and benevolent, and that the cross affirms that God is love. Spiritual intelligence reveals God in the world through living a life consistent with the cross of Christ.

> [27] *Whoever does not carry the cross and follow me cannot be my disciple.*
>
> LUKE 14:27

The wisdom of the world was not capable of grasping the wisdom of God. The wisdom of God was hidden by the wisdom of the world. To possess the wisdom that comes from God will open the eyes of the spiritual person to the lies of the world's constructs of wisdom. I am now using the word "world" as it is used in the Johannine literature to speak of human constructs of social realities.

The spiritually intelligent person then is sensitive to the evil in the world based upon their sentient and intellectual relationship with God and the scriptures. The evil can no longer hide from the light. Although the spiritual person seeks understanding on the relationship of the just God and the unjust world, the spiritual person does not find an answer. The task of acting in the world consistent with the revelation of God in Christ on the cross becomes a lived wisdom.

> Sensitivity to evil is evidence of spiritual awareness. Seeking to overcome evil with good is bearing the burden of reality. Fearlessly articulating truth's critique on the present age, while proclaiming the story of redemption, with the possibility of losing one's life, is culpability and spiritual intelligence.

The spiritually intelligent person, due to the integration of sentience and intellect, is aware of evil and then begins to carry the burden of their knowledge. Their burden will move on to overcoming the evil with good. Evil is not overcome merely by ideological arguments, but by acts that reveal goodness; that is God.

Finally, the spiritually intelligent person will take the final step and carry their cross; they will recognize their own culpability as a human being in the world and become living reenactments of Jesus in their particular life.

This can be read as the ABCs of spiritual intelligence, that is, awareness, burden, and culpability. Briefly, spiritual intelligence begins with the concept of a good and benevolent God and is the outcome of learning to integrate sentience and intellect in the pursuit of God and comes to mature fruition through the movements of awareness, burden, and culpability.

Sensitivity to evil is evidence of spiritual awareness. Seeking to overcome evil with good is bearing the burden of reality. Fearlessly articulating truth's critique on the present age, while proclaiming the story of redemption, with the possibility of losing one's life, is culpability and spiritual maturity.

Reading Twenty-One

Responsible Faith

Caring for Creation

God is infinite but the resources of the created world are limited. It is a mistake to suppose that God will create a new resource from nothing. We are responsible for the consumption of the earth's resources. The flourishing of life is dependent upon how we live in relation to others, in relation to the ground. The ability of human beings to explore the created world through scientific efforts born of imagination is still before us with expansive opportunity. However, the ethical acquisition of wealth is as important as the ethical use of power achieved through science and technology. Creation responds to moral living while death continues its grip on reality. This is Christian theology. We are called to enter into the rest of God. The continued work of God in creation is to bring humanity into this rest; it is the story of salvation in history. Jesus' teaching on the kingdom of God is synonymous with the writer of Hebrews' conception of rest, with John's concept of eternal life, with Paul's understanding of being in Christ. Salvation is more than a personal matter for the individual; salvation is the work of God for all of humanity, for every aspect of human life, including the manner in which we consume the earth's resources.

Responsibility

God is not restricted by some unwritten law; rather, God is responsible for the communication of God's self and for determining humanity's responsibility under the sun. The instruction of God within the structures of reality is not disrupted at the whims of human attempts to acquire wealth without effort, without ethical living. The unethical acquisition of wealth is always disruptive to human life and is a form of violence. For this reason the revelation of God in history is played out against the backdrop of consistency in nature (Gen 9:9–17).

In the gospels, Jesus multiplies loaves and fishes, and feeds thousands with a boy's lunch. Certainly this is the creation of food; however, this is not an act for personal gain but a sign of Jesus as a Prophet like Moses (even greater than Moses). Also, the multiplication of food to be consumed is not like creating oil where the geological processes of time have not been present. It does not seem that this sign of Jesus is a multiplication of resources from nothing in order to enrich a person or change the creation, but the multiplication of food for a moment in order to affirm his life and teaching. The signs in the life of Jesus serve to draw attention to his person, life, and teaching. The multiplication of the loaves and fishes are a picture of Jesus feeding the masses as Moses did in the wilderness. No one has accomplished such a sign since Jesus. The uniqueness of Jesus is that he is the *monogenes;* the only begotten.

> [30] *Now Jesus did many other signs in the presence of his disciples, which are not written in this book.* [31] *But these are written so that you may come to believe that Jesus is the Messiah, the Son of God, and that through believing you may have life in his name.*
>
> JOHN 20:30–31

Throughout Scripture there is a teaching that claims our moral and ethical behavior affects the earth, the land. The expulsion from the garden results in a hostile environment that produces thorns and thistles and makes tilling the ground more difficult. That oft-repeated piece from Chronicles affirms this idea.

> [14] *if my people who are called by my name humble themselves, pray, seek my face, and turn from their wicked ways, then I will hear from heaven, and will forgive their sin and heal their land.*
>
> 2 CHR 7:14

Although this theological ideology is found throughout Scripture, it carries some baggage that Jesus corrects.

> [44] *But I say to you, Love your enemies and pray for those who persecute you,* [45] *so that you may be children of your Father in heaven; for*

> *he makes his sun rise on the evil and on the good, and sends rain on the righteous and on the unrighteous.*
>
> MATT 5:44–45

Likewise, catastrophe falls on the righteous and the unrighteous. So, although our moral and ethical behaviors affect the earth, judging the morality of a people based upon natural disaster is problematic. God blesses the earth with rain that benefits both righteous and unrighteous. Nonetheless, repentance and morality, coupled with ethical living, produce healthy harvests.

> ² *Swearing, lying, and murder, and stealing and adultery break out; bloodshed follows bloodshed.* ³ *Therefore the land mourns, and all who live in it languish; together with the wild animals and the birds of the air, even the fish of the sea are perishing.*
>
> HOSEA 4:2–3

I think we should understand that when moral communities of faith live ethically, then life flourishes. This is our connection to the ground; greed, violence, and murder disrupt the cultivation of life.

In our modern age, we have learned to use technology and science to ensure the mass production of food and are separated from the ground. Nonetheless, the languishing of nature is a sign of the immorality present in humanity. The healing of the earth requires that we all turn to the voice of God, and the earth becomes God's sanctuary, filled with his Spirit-indwelt children.

The healing of the earth and the flourishing of nature does not require the creation of new resources but the care of humanity, as we learn how to live in relation to one another and responsibly consume the earth's (God's) provisions.

There is a tension in the teaching of Jesus on the kingdom of God. This tension is a mixture of immediacy and hope for a day yet to come—the now/not yet concept. The call is to live as though the reign of God is already active, and to do so in the face of death, even in a world blind to the reality for which it is headed. In effect, all believers carry within their hearts a utopian ideal for which we are responsible to live out within the confines of a world that is set in opposition to our understanding.

I think the consummation of the utopian ideal results in the complete rejection of violence, which is an act of spiritual maturation. The nonviolent death of Christian martyrs is a witness and reminder of the broken powers of death, which were defeated when Jesus rose from the grave.

When a disciple of Jesus begins to see the world as a person whose eyes penetrate the darkness like light, then their presence in the now is disruptive to the powers of darkness and those pesky perennial idols of militarism, materialism, and ethnocentrism (nationalism) all pale in comparison to the glorious vision of God indwelling humanity. Truly we are meant to be one—one organism—alive in Christ (in God), each functioning in love and free from the terror of death's claim to finality.

The rest of God is the faith of God, a faith so grand that the chaos of existence is seen as conquered, healed, and transformed, because he is Lord. Jesus has invited us into this rest; it is rest in the midst of hopelessness, simply because God is Lord over all creation.

History is reversed and every wound healed, every tear touched with grace, as we enter into eternal life (now and forever).

Reading Twenty-Two

Adam's Lament

She was walking in our garden
a blossom of love
a feeling in my soul knew she had come from above
she saw beauty in all that gave life
longing to taste of all that was good
she sought to understand the world we were in
but something went wrong O Lord something went wrong
a sword pierced my soul as we wandered outside the garden of love.
You O Lord presented her as gift and all your gifts are good.

Sorrow

In the text, Eve's act is not a moral failure. It is not a sin that is a moral violation of good (unless good is understood to be God). The tree is not evil, nor is it magical; the only difference between this tree and all the others is a prohibition placed upon eating its fruit. Eve looks for a reason to refrain from partaking of the tree and concludes that there is no valid reason. The fruit is aesthetically pleasing to the eye, ethically she understands it is good for food like all the other trees, plus it contains the path to becoming like God: to know good and evil. Isn't this the pursuit of religion—to know God and to discern good from evil?

So she acts contrary to the prohibition from Yahweh. Her failure to obey the voice of Yahweh, even when there is no good reason to do so (except that prohibition which she must have learned from Adam), is in effect the end of the mythical paradise. The story is instructive. As human beings, we refuse to restrain ourselves from exploring any and all of creation. The desire held at the center of our thoughts is to overcome the hostility of the world and fight death.

In the absence of God, Eve seeks to gain knowledge, which is the prohibited desire and ability of humanity to reach beyond the voice of God and defy the underlying structures of reality. The inner voice of God in the moral conscience and the structures of reality serve to restrain humanity's ability to take dominion over creation to their own harm. We suffer at our own hands as we reach beyond the voice of God in creation and defy the underlying moral, ethical, and ecological structures of reality.

The story is about human beings accepting their limits within a garden, where all is pronounced good (even the forbidden tree). The only limit that is set is, in a sense, a false limit, for the tree is only a tree. The prohibition, however, is Yahweh's instructive lesson. The tree of the knowledge of good and evil is humanity's ever-present desire to reach beyond the limits Yahweh has placed. Humanity fails to rest as creature in relation to the creator, humanity wants equality with the creator to speak and act as a child of the creator and not merely a creature. In effect, the human beings have become self-destructive; they have grasped at God within the context of creation (the garden) and have not learned to live properly in relation to him. As I write I am thinking of Michelangelo's picture of man reaching to touch God, as a child, as an equal.

The mythical paradise is an imagined moment when humanity, created in the image of God, began their journey away from God. Outside the garden they are pressed under the constraint of mortality, suffering, pain, and horrendous evil. Their experience has revealed death as the ultimate impassable limit, the final word. Humanity will recognize God (Yahweh); the journey is not vain. From the position of suffering and pain, humanity will now reach for God, seeking release from an existence that is intolerable, severe in judgment, unimaginable in its spiral towards death. However, the Creator, Yahweh, will also reach for humanity and provide them with what they need: a relationship with God as father. The chasm between God and humanity will be bridged by God's self.

> The chasm between God and humanity will be bridged by God's self.

It is a strange but gripping story, for east of Eden life has become mixed with death. Death has not come immediately, but rather as a pervasive force, permeating humanity like a parasitic invasion. Death, as God's greatest judgment, ends humanity's hope to live forever and pursue God within the confines of creation. God is more than the creation. This is where faith and transcendence become part of human language.

Death is now the obstacle between God and humanity. The creature has been stricken with the frightful reality of creaturely limitations. Yes, sin is an obstacle, but sin has become inevitable east of Eden. Outside the mythical paradise, all partake of sin. Sin is not merely individual failure but existential reality. Many sins enter the world and the voice of God is no longer a simple prohibition; it includes the presence of death.

> God must reveal God's self, for humanity does not know him.

This is compatible with God's agreement with the Israelites at the mountain.

> [23] *When you heard the voice out of the darkness, while the mountain was burning with fire, you approached me, all the heads of your tribes and your elders;* [24] *and you said, "Look, the LORD our God has shown us his glory and greatness, and we have heard his voice out of the fire. Today we have seen that God may speak to someone and the person may still live.* [25] *So now why should we die? For this great fire will consume us; if we hear the voice of the LORD our God any longer, we shall die.* [26] *For who is there of all flesh that has heard the voice of the living God speaking out of fire, as we have, and remained alive?* [27] *Go near, you yourself, and hear all that the LORD our God will say. Then tell us everything that the LORD our God tells you, and we will listen and do it."* [28] *The LORD heard your words when you spoke to me, and the LORD said to me: "I have heard the words of this people, which they have spoken to you; they are right in all that they have spoken.*
>
> DEUT 5:23-28

There will have to be a change, a change in God that bridges the chasm, a change in humanity that embraces their creatureliness. Of course, God does not change in character; it is God's nature to be holy. However, there will be in salvation history a dramatic change in God, for he will join the creation and become a human being (Phil 2:5-11). God will make the creation a part of himself, but that part of creation that will be united into the transcendent holy one will be humanity. The last Adam, who left an empty tomb, has replaced the first Adam, expelled from the mythical garden. For this reason, humanity must also change, not only in accepting creatureliness, but also in accepting God as King—a King to be obeyed, a Lord whose supremacy is unmistakable and unchallengeable.

More than a voice to be obeyed, God reveals himself to be love—the holy one who defines morality, the Lord of life whose desire is for all of humanity to receive his gift of life, to become like God the Son. Now humanity can reach for God and live within the limits of creation without the desire to defy those limits, for God has become their desire. God has reached for humanity and embraced them into his very being, giving them what they lacked, an indivisible relationship of co-existence with God because God gave more of God's self than was present at the beginning in the garden.

Reading Twenty-Three

Jesus and the Roman Tax

An Unnatural Sign

A Fish cannot eat a coin, nor can a Man
With mocking reluctance God returns to Caesar a coin
The voice of the poor chokes on the hypocrisy of Caesar's justice
Jesus' invitation is liberation
A game of miracles
A Kingdom without Currency

Who Owns the Fish of the Sea?

The gospel story of Jesus' response to religious leaders questioning his stance on taxation is over taxes imposed upon a subjugated people living under the power of an empire. This being said, applying these stories as theological responses about Jesus' teaching on taxes levied on people by their own government is inconsistent with the situation of Israel under Roman rule. Although both cases in the gospels are in the context of taxation imposed by a foreign power, they reflect Jesus' understanding of money and power. I will address the two gospel stories that record Jesus' response to taxation by empire.

It seems that Jesus' lessons on taxation are not a simple affirmation of legitimacy. Rather, Jesus views taxation as something to be tolerated in order to avoid unnecessary conflict. When Jesus pays taxes with a coin extracted from a fish's mouth, we must consider the dichotomy. Peter derives a living by fishing. God made fish and fish are given freely to the man willing to capture them in his net. Caesar makes money and attaches it to that which God has created and given to humanity. A coin does not belong in the mouth of a fish. A coin cannot feed a fish or a man. So Jesus performs a miracle, a sign act, and a coin is pulled from a fish's mouth to satisfy the parasitical hunger of Caesar to live off that which God has freely given to fishermen. Jesus tells Peter that as a child of God he is free, but in order to avoid offending the subjugating power of empire, he must pay the tax. The lesson is clear: as a disciple, Peter has more important work than resisting taxation. In order to fulfill his task he must live as a free man who voluntarily submits to taxation in order to preach the good news of God in Christ without (needlessly) offending the temporary powers of Caesar over money.

In another story, dealing with this theme of taxation by Caesar, we see the efforts of some of Jesus' religious competitors, seeking to make quick work of Jesus by exposing him as a tax resistor—a political zealot, refusing to honor Caesar.

> [22] *Is it lawful for us to pay taxes to the emperor, or not?"* [23] *But he perceived their craftiness and said to them,* [24] *"Show me a denarius. Whose head and whose title does it bear?" They said, "The emperor's."* [25] *He said to them, "Then give to the emperor the things that are the emperor's, and to God the things that are God's."* [26] *And they were not able in the presence of the people to trap him by what he said; and being amazed by his answer, they became silent.*
>
> LUKE 20:22–26

However, Jesus quickly exposes the hypocrisy of his detractors, for they possess the coinage of Caesar in abundance and Jesus must ask one of them to show him a coin. Jesus' lesson is that the coin bears the image of its creator, Caesar. So, Jesus responds by telling them to give to Caesar that which Caesar has created after his own image. And give to God that which is God's. Well, everything belongs to God, including Caesar; in fact all human beings belong to God for they are created in his image. In Jesus' teaching, people are more important than money. To attempt to murder Jesus by proxy (through Caesar and trickery), his religious competitors are exposed as idolaters and murderers.

The creation of diverse nations through natural boundaries and language is God's effort to limit the ability of man to rule over the entire earth from a centralized position of power (Genesis 11). This division of humanity is portrayed and accomplished by divine fiat. It is through language that the development of culture and the freedom to search for God within each people group is established (Acts 17:26–27). In this sense, the nation-state is closer to God's efforts than empire. However, the Bible's history on the birthing of the nation-state teaches that in the process of seeking a king (president) the people reject the reign of God (1 Samuel 8). So, living within the constraints of national government is (until his kingdom comes) the inevitable condition of humanity at large, with the exception being some tribal groups.

> This story is not about Jesus legitimizing the taxation of empire; it is about being wise enough to stay alive and not die over money.

The law of Israel was to provide for the people a way of living together which was conducive to humans flourishing. Further, the law was understood to be instructive, more than absolute. So capital punishment for various crimes was real, but subject to mercy; it had more value as teaching than practice. The Torah comes about due to Israel's inability to hear the living voice of Yahweh. So the Decalogue alone is insufficient, more law is needed (Deut 5:23–33). Law then is the governing instrument for humanity, and governing human beings must enforce law. As a people, it was God's intention that Israel as a people be known for her flourishing, due to a love for law—law that was to be instructive and reveal God (merciful, gracious, slow to anger, forgiving [Exod 34:6]). In a government of law the service of the king is to reflect God in behavior and live according to the law (Deut 17:14–20).

A just society is governed by law that alleviates poverty, and seeks the welfare of all its citizens. Our laws are more important than our king (president). The tax burden is necessary for the adjudication of law; the problem is that our leaders use their power to tax for war and expansion rather than the maintenance of life and peace. For this reason we should pay our taxes while keeping the right to question how taxes are collected and how the monetary resources of the nation are spent. A just nation also preserves the right of citizens to dissent through legal and peaceful means. So, life under the sun is always a struggle for the reign of God.

The abuse of law by legislators is a sin against humanity and God. God speaks through the contemplative effort of law-making within the complexity of human experience. Law is to be accompanied with the Spirit of grace that seeks good for all. Israel's laws may seem archaic, from a less civilized era, but within the construct of grace we can find teaching that looks at the reason for the law. Laws regulate human behavior; we do bad and cannot be stopped. However, the damage we cause can be regulated with law.

Reading Twenty-Four

Ending Poverty by Becoming Human

The Poor

The smile of the poor can never heal the pain it hides
The smile shouts I'm alive, I'm people
A tear for a smile, a blind eye for your pain
Are we invisible or is your smile a lie?

Evil and Poverty

Poverty has a number of causes: illness, war, natural disasters, illiteracy, lack of access to education, for-profit penal institutions, development in the name of progress that does not address the rights of settled or indigenous people, and displacement caused by all of the aforementioned.

However, only when civilization recognizes poverty as a systemic evil— an evil sustained by injustice, ethnocentrism, and the belief that the unlimited acquisition of wealth is an ideology that must be defended with violence— will we begin to adequately address the challenge of eradicating poverty.

Capitalism is not a divine system for governing economic affairs. The Jewish people attempted to control unregulated capitalism with debt-forgiveness and land-restoration; this is the Christian heritage. Unfortunately, we forgive the wealthy elite for the unethical acquisition of wealth, while holding the poor captive to unrelenting debt.

We will always have the poor with us, Jesus said. Yet I think Jesus' hope would be that poverty would be alleviated, when it is within the human potential to do so. I do not think Jesus intended that we are to accept poverty as a permanent condition for any person or peoples. Rather, I think

Jesus viewed poverty as a temporary condition to be corrected by all the powers we can gather through the political, the social, the church, and the neighbor (ultimately by the establishing of the kingdom of God).

The capitalist system works by way of the myth of progress in technological and structural systems. Some technological progress aids life and is essential; some is uselessly unethical and destructive to life. Our technological and structural progress does not make us better human beings. This is the myth: that progress will produce better human beings. So along the way we must sacrifice others to the cause of progress.

If we are to judge progress, we must do so by removing violence from the equation; this is the way of God. Human progress accomplished at the expense of human life is nothing more than a cyclical eruption of violence that ultimately results in devaluing life. Violence will erupt again and our progress becomes more and more dangerous to life until we now threaten the very planet on which we were created to live.

The Christian faith challenges the ease with which we sacrifice people to progress; we are our brother's keepers. We are not here to rape the earth, but to care for the intricate ecosystem that God has put in place. Death's voice is not final; the one person that lived a completely full human life in harmony with God was resurrected. Mortality is no longer solely determinate; it has been interrupted.

To be a moral human being and to live ethically in the sight of God and humanity is the epitome of human progress and has more power to change reality than any discovery ever made by science. So, we look back at the great souls that have graced human history and lift up those that stood for peace and nonviolence. Even those anti-pluralist, exclusive Christians use Ghandi as a model for Christian living. Perhaps he knew Jesus in a better way than many a divisive, mean-spirited "born-again Christian."

We deify our constitution and as fine a document as it is, it is not Scripture. We deify our political system as the closest thing we can get to God, yet this is untrue for he calls us closer and holds us accountable for systemic evil in the sociopolitical spheres of life. We deify our institutions and our ideologies in order to ignore the call of God to eradicate the suffering of humanity caused by those very institutions and ideologies.

Am I a utopian? Am I a progressive seeking a better world? Am I a contrarian always seeking a point of view differing from the status quo? No. I am a Christian that flees the idolatry of nationalism, ethnocentrism, militarism, and materialism, seeking first the kingdom of God.

Reading Twenty-Five

The American Oligarchy

> For scoundrels are found among my people;
> they take over the goods of others.
> Like fowlers they set a trap;
> they catch human beings.
> Like a cage full of birds,
> their houses are full of treachery;
> therefore they have become great and rich,
> they have grown fat and sleek.
> They know no limits in deeds of wickedness;
> they do not judge with justice the cause of the orphan,
> to make it prosper, and they do not defend the rights of the needy.
> Shall I not punish them for these things? says the LORD,
> and shall I not bring retribution on a nation such as this?
> JER 5:26–29

Wealth and Social Stratification

The American Oligarchy is consciously eroding away the vestiges of democracy through a new form of government whose foundational goal and supporting ideology is profit for the few, and whose vehicle for power is the corporation. For example, when an American corporation based in Tennessee begins to buy up American prisons for the sake of making money and turns this business into an international effort that reaches into other nations, it is evident that we are approaching an era of unprecedented power, held by non-elected officials, whose power is built into the laws that support economic control of institutions free from representation of the people.

America must face the realization that unlimited personal wealth is an unethical way for human beings to govern the resources of the world. Interestingly, the practice of limiting wealth acquisition is a biblical concept. Deuteronomy 15 is the record of an alleged primitive people whose leader had enough insight into human economic practices that he penned legislation for limiting the acquisition of personal wealth and the forgiveness of debt, in order to halt both greed and the oppressive nature of poverty. The legislation is applied universally to society, regardless of whether poverty is a result of illness, catastrophe, bad business deals, or society's failure to lift up her neediest members with education and opportunity. It is the revelation of ethical monotheism that guided Israel's scribal community to produce these writings that speak across the millennia. This Torah legislation is consistent with the teaching of Jesus and embodies the heart of Jesus' kingdom in practical governance.

I am using the phrase "personal wealth" because in our age the corporation's need for capital to be exchanged through a negotiable medium is necessary. However, the corporations of the world must be governed by legislation that requires ethically humane practices. Corporations must be of service to the people of the earth. America's interest is not a guiding ethic for humanity. America's interest, at present, is to ensure the ongoing acquisition of wealth and power, regardless of the detrimental effects this interest has on other nations. Taxing the wealthy oligarchy is not the solution; it is merely a bandage. Rather, the governing of corporations with humanitarian ethics and the limiting of personal wealth acquired through corporate activity is essential for change. Further, limiting personal wealth and the periodic forgiving of personal and national debt is a workable Judeo-Christian concept that should be supported by the church.

Of course, the problem is money is a complex power. How are businesses to grow unless investors are motivated to contribute to the business enterprise? I suggest that if personal wealth is limited, the need to include the small investor would serve to regulate inhumane corporate activity and greed. Further, small investors can look forward to a growing potential for economic security over the course of life. After all, the payouts to corporate executives are enough to provide retirement for America's seniors and disabled.

In contemporary Christianity we need to learn how to apply the teaching of Jesus. For instance, Jesus made it clear that the person of faith has an attitude of hatred towards money.

> [13] *No slave can serve two masters; for a slave will either hate the one and love the other, or be devoted to the one and despise the other. You cannot serve God and wealth."*
>
> LUKE 16:13

Jesus' teaching that money is a master to be hated, places money outside the realm of the reign of God as a power that genders injustice. Jesus does not advocate an immediate eradication of the monetary system; rather, his instruction is on the power of money to compete with and overcome the voice of God. This being said, the believer's attitude toward money is an educated awareness of the power of money to circumvent the reign of God in the earth. Living in the now/not yet reality of the Kingdom of God, believers must contend with temporary powers like money. The role of the church is to manifest this attitude towards money and it should be taught, even preached from the pulpit.

> Jesus' teaching that money is a master to be hated places money outside the realm of the reign of God as a power that genders injustice.

In practice, the limiting of personal wealth is accomplished by ethical business models that look to the welfare of employees within the business enterprise. In the book of Acts, the utopian sharing of wealth through disposal proved to be a failed experiment, for it resulted in the poverty of the Jerusalem church. When a community divests itself of tangible assets, it is left subject to poverty. The maintenance of wealth for the benefit of others is a practice to be balanced with a self-discipline that refuses to live with opulence.

Money is a power that separates people, even families. Learning to live with money as a real need, established by temporary powers, is as important as learning how to live in ways that promote well-being without dependence upon money. This type of discipline is found in the church's ability to help one another. For example, a plumber repairs the home of a struggling family at no charge; an ophthalmologist provides free services for those persons that live at an economic level which prohibits their success in society. This kind of activity requires a church that promotes community awareness sharing. There are many ways to enable the institutional church to become an intentional community. For example, storytelling contributes to the communal development of culture. The kind of storytelling we need is dependent upon identifying the persons gifted with this art. This kind of culture-developing communal storytelling requires people with years of experience who can relate a story in such a way that it defines moral ambiguity with active response. This type of storytelling is, most often, accounts from a person's experience. Rather than movie attendance, storytelling nights can engage a community of people in a healthy way that is both entertaining and challenging.

Storytelling nights need to allow for the presence of all ages. Children are exposed to the stories of the Bible without complaint (perhaps this practice needs to be questioned). However, storytelling requires guidance by the storyteller and the parents. Storytelling events are not a place for overly sensitive parents. The storyteller should not be censored for the subject matter, but the attendees should be informed. Children grow up in this world and adults learn quickly how shielding children from the violence of the world is only a temporary solution. A home where openness and conversation enable parents to guide their children leaves the judgment to the parents to determine whether a subject is beyond the child's maturation and cognitive emotional skills.

People need to take back the power of the story that has been co-opted by the entertainment industry. Storytelling is a very human act; it is a cultural building foundation for humane living that unites the generations. Perhaps it felt odd to read this piece as it turned to storytelling. I did this because the regaining of culture by the people is an essential part of restoring humanity.

Without an alternative culture-building community, Christianity becomes compromised and accommodates the powers of the present age. In our era Christianity has contributed to the idol of democratic capitalism as the end of history.

Reading Twenty-Six

Josiah's Failed Reforms and the Book of Jonah

Repentance

Legislating morality—impossible
Regulating behavior—violent
Social change comes from below
The Halls of Power are Corrupt
If my People
Hear God—Resist the Powers

Lessons in Governing

The reforms of Josiah are understood by biblical scholars to have been a failure; this is so for numerous reasons. The ministry of Jeremiah and others overlap with the time frame of Josiah's efforts to enforce religious reform upon the people. It is apparent the people did not internalize the religious fervor depicted by the effort of Josiah. This is so because at the outset of Jeremiah's ministry he delivers his "Temple Sermon" recorded in Jeremiah chapters 7 and 26, in which the people are called to repentance. The sermon in chapter 26 suggests that God would change his mind about the Babylonian assault and exile, if the people repent. The seeming religious zealousness of the time was extrinsic in nature and not intrinsic; they were not reflections of the heart.

In chapter 7, the people have apparently adopted a chant of two words in Hebrew (temple Yahweh). When two nouns are placed in construct in

Hebrew, then the preposition "of" is placed between the two words. The grammatical term for two nouns placed side by side is "construct," meaning the two nouns are connected with an unspoken preposition, e.g. Temple of Yahweh. So, the people were chanting for the restoration of the temple. Unfortunately, their fervor was external and political, not internal and spiritual. So, Jeremiah calls their chant a lie; without the internal repentance the temple is useless, an unacceptable place of worship.

Likewise, it is apparent in the book of Jeremiah that although Josiah removed the sacred trees (*asherah*), the people quickly reconstructed the sites for their immoral activities, they also continued sacrificing their children to Moloch (Jer 7:31) and praying to the Queen of Heaven (Jer 7:18). In effect, Josiah's reforms failed because they were merely efforts to legislate religion through the power of a king or by way of political power.

Although legislation is always an effort to regulate human behavior for producing a moral society, the power of legislation cannot change the human heart. This is the problem with understanding Josiah's reform as a great revival; it supposes that political force and coercion is sufficient to change the hearts of people. This is the error of much of the evangelical political rhetoric we hear today—a practice which leads to the idolatry of nationalism.

The book of Jonah serves well to make this point. Part of the purpose of Jonah is to both present and expose the problem as to why God destroyed Jerusalem and spared Nineveh. The dating of Jonah is (of course) subject to debate, but regardless of the date, Jonah serves canonically to provide an answer to the dilemma of Israel's slaughter by the Babylonians and subsequent exile in comparison to the graciousness of God to spare Nineveh. Josiah's reforms came from the top down. Josiah tried to serve well as an exemplar, which is the duty of every Israelite king (Deut 17:14–20). Likewise, in the developing messianic understanding, the scribes of Israel consistently sought to identify the messianic hope with their kings, thus the strong words of approval upon Josiah's efforts.

Whereas Josiah's efforts through political force failed to produce repentance (the necessary element for revival), the story of Jonah in Nineveh reports that repentance began with the people and made its way up to the king (Jonah 3:4–6). This is an important lesson for the church. We cannot rely upon political power to produce a moral society.

The church is always subjected to the temptation of structural power in government and society. This is so because law governs us and law has a profound effect upon the civility, health, and morality of a society.

Although morality cannot be legislated into the hearts of people, morality can, through legislation, be encultured as an accepted norm for behavior and thus affect the way people live. However, the appearance of morality as accepted encultured behavior leaves the human heart untouched.

It is good and right that the church be concerned with morality and social justice. The issue is where the church is to position her efforts in relation to the constructs of power that govern the nation-state. First, the church is to be in Christ whose kingdom is not compatible with the present structures of human governing. This places the church alongside the poor, who are powerless in the world and their voices are not heard. The church is to give voice for suffering humanity in compassion and peace. Jesus' vision of the reign of God is a creative transformation of reality that begins in the heart.

> Without the maturation of God's people, the present age will not experience the reality of the reign of God.

Reading Twenty-Seven

A Missional Reading of Luke's Pentecost Narrative

Language

God's rebuke to Empire
An indomitable Phenomenon
Erupting from the cultural soul of a people
God's call to God's People
A multilingual challenge of love

Indomitable Language

³ After his suffering he presented himself alive to them by many convincing proofs, appearing to them during forty days and speaking about the kingdom of God. ⁴ While staying with them, he ordered them not to leave Jerusalem, but to wait there for the promise of the Father. "This," he said, "is what you have heard from me; ⁵ for John baptized with water, but you will be baptized with the Holy Spirit not many days from now."

ACTS 1:3–5

Although my focus in this essay will be on the Pentecost narrative of Acts chapter 2, I will approach Luke's work as that of a theologian whose reporting of events produces a structurally connected theological narrative through the entirety of his book. I understand Luke's writing to be subversive art and missionally-oriented instruction for Theophilus and all who seek to grasp the message of Luke as narrative theology. Although understanding the sociocultural aspects of the people about whom Luke writes is important, social science readings can be restrictive and miss the imagination of an author whose understanding and message of the events he is reporting is universally applicable beyond the setting in which they occur.

Chapter 2 of Acts begins with the waiting persons of chapter 1 who numbered about 120. In obedience to Jesus' order (Acts 1:4), the apostles and the early Jesus-followers are all waiting for an empowering event, a reception of Spirit that enables them to be the message bearers of Jesus' life, teaching, and resurrection. Chapter 2 of Acts is the reporting of this event. In John's gospel those persons born of the Spirit are unpredictable and uncontainable, like the wind. It is fitting that the descent of the Spirit from above (heaven) manifests as a powerful wind representing the unpredictable, uncontainable presence and power of God.

During this apparently loud and disruptive moment, there is a vision of fiery tongues dividing off and landing on each of the gathered company. They begin to speak in other languages and Luke insists that this is accomplished through the active effort of the Spirit. Luke desires that his reader understand that when the Spirit of God arrives, the boundaries of language are breached as a part of God's missional effort with humanity. The other persons present, (Hebrews of the Diaspora) who had been born in other parts of the world, hear Galileans speak in the languages of the lands from which the listeners had traveled.

In relation to the Babel story of Genesis 11, Acts 2 affirms the work of God to birth nations through the division of languages. Like many stories in Genesis, the Babel story serves as an etiology, in this case for the origin of languages. The Babel story is understood to oppose the attempts of empire to centralize power and rule over humanity. God has made human beings in such a way that we give birth to languages as a cultural phenomenon; language births culture and culture births language. Language binds us together like the Spirit. The Pentecost story of Acts is God's missional response to the Judeans present at the descent of the Spirit. God desires to speak to all nations through those persons filled with the Spirit. In this case, he's speaking particularly to those persons present, who hear because they know the languages of the nations.

The nations do not need to learn Hebrew (or Latin) in order to know God, for God has sanctified the use of their language by speaking to each of them through the persons receiving the Spirit during Pentecost. Further, because culture and language are bound together inextricably, culture likewise is sanctified. It is not that God approves all aspects of any culture; rather, it is that God embraces the diversity of humanity as his doing, his work. Even as culture and language are inextricably immersed in one another, so God is beginning to inextricably immerse humanity with God's self through the Spirit.

> The Babel story is God's aversion to any form of governing that attempts to place all peoples under its power.

What does this event mean to those persons that heard the languages of their homelands being spoken by Galileans? It means that God has prepared them to return and speak "God's deeds of power" in the language and culture of those whom they live among. The 3,000 persons added to the believers comprised those dispersed Jews that had made the pilgrimage to Jerusalem. They would return as witnesses, as missionaries. The first missionaries had learned the foreign languages they spoke through natural means (there is no indication that the Galileans who spoke in languages during Pentecost retained or learned the languages they praised God in). This also provides a missional paradigm for the church today. We must teach our missionaries the languages of the people they serve and not depend upon the power of empire to dictate a single language or culture. The work of God is universal and not confined to the Temple in Jerusalem, nor are pilgrimages to Jerusalem consistent with the work of God. The dispersion of the Judeans by the Babylonians effectively prepared a group of people to become missionaries to the rest of the nations.

This missional aspect of Luke's second volume is played out structurally to communicate a theological truth: a people are defined by their language and culture, but God is not confined to any language or culture. Effectively, God is turning Israel into a nation of priests. In order to serve the other nations, they suffered dispersion, but it had prepared them to communicate across the boundaries of language and culture. Luke will resist the dominance of a few, even the apostles. At the beginning of chapter 6 the apostles think themselves so grand that they cannot attend to the needs of widows. In chapter 8, Saul, the consummate Jew, the ambitious religionist, is making it his business to eliminate the universal effort to make God's presence and Spirit available for the nations. In between these stories (chapter 7) is the Hellenist Stephen, whose testimony and martyrdom result in a vision of Jesus standing to honor him. The standing of Jesus is significant because of the New Testament's use of Psalm 110 in which Jesus is seated.

Stephen the Hellenist serves so well that Jesus honors him. Stephen is filled with grace and power, whereas Peter is given grace. The outsider

Stephen has become the model, the one that looks the most like Jesus. Peter has been overcome; I think that when people were healed by Peter's shadow it was unhealthy for Peter. Peter, like Saul, seems to be interested in becoming a man of religious power and influence. Peter oversees the death of Ananias and Sapphira and Saul oversees the death of Stephen; they are both failing. The Spirit of God and the Lord Jesus were manifested through a Greek-speaking Jew. The Jesus movement is not to be contained by religious powers centered in Jerusalem (or Rome).

As the day of Pentecost unfolds, Peter steps up to clarify the meaning of the events and turns to a piece of Scripture from the book of Joel. Joel's spiritual eschaton is marked by an egalitarian reception of God's spirit, not only men or priests, but young and old, sons and daughters, slaves and women, partake in the presence of God to prophesy and experience dreams and visions. Peter argues further through the use of Joel (from silence since everyone there knows) that the signs of fire seen that day, the darkness and the earthquake at the time of Christ's crucifixion, are all part of those events that denote the appearance of God.

Peter continues his sermon and argues effectively that Jesus was greater than David—that Jesus is a superior model, a national hero of greater measure than David. This is so because David is dead and Jesus is alive. The shock for all of those hearing Peter's sermon is that the Messiah is nothing like David: not a conqueror, not a man of war, not interested in centralizing power in order to ensure his will is accomplished. The resurrection and the giving of the Spirit are both affirmations of the truth that Jesus is Lord and Messiah. Jesus is seated at God's right hand waiting for his enemies to be made a stool for his feet. It is evident that the enemies of Jesus are not like David's enemies; rather the enemies of Jesus are all forms of human depravity. God is working in the world and a nonviolent crucified man who has ascended into heaven and whose body does not decay, accomplishes salvation; he has power over our greatest enemy, death.

The burgeoning movement of Spirit-filled Jesus-followers experiences some rapid growth. In their innocence and fervor they sell their possessions and lose their economic base. This social experiment will result in Paul's need to raise money for *the poor*, which will be a synonym for the Jerusalem church. Luke's record of the early church reveals well-meaning apostles and people who make mistakes and fail even in the midst of spiritual renewal. The day of Pentecost, the descent, and giving of the Spirit indicate that God desires to save all humanity and opposes structures of power that exalt individual human beings, or one nation over another.

Reading Twenty-Eight

God's Imagination

Before God Spoke
Imagination pictured creation
I tried to imagine something no one had ever seen
Impossible
I chose to believe in the one no one had ever seen

Imagining with God

The Divine imagination is responsible for all creation, all existence. Every idea that forms reality was conceived in God's imagination. To ascribe eternal existence to the ideas that form reality is to deify human perceptions of truth and to deny the imagination of the creator; this is the idolatry of Platonism. To ascribe to God an omniscience void of imaginative creative events results in a static reductionist theology that robs God of holiness (his nature) and personhood (his ontological existence).

The divine imagination is guided by insight and wisdom. Insight and wisdom are properties of God's being, attributes of his person, and tools of his creative imagination and work.

> [22] The LORD possessed me in the beginning of his way, before his works of old . . . [24] When there were no depths I was brought forth, when there were no springs abounding with water.
>
> PROV 8:22, 24

The possession of wisdom precedes the creative event and is descriptive of God's imagination at work. Wisdom's appearance in the work of creation is communicated as a birthing through use of the word *holalti*, which refers to the writhing anguish of childbirth. The birth language associated with wisdom's appearance is indicative of the function of imagination as exploratory thought. Creation is a great adventure as unpredictable as a child. Wisdom is God's great discovery that enables him to join humanity's conscious becoming.

An omniscience that is void of imagination and event is not a biblically supportable theology. The philosophical concept of possible worlds in relation to omniscience seems to be infinitely redundant, imposing upon God needless absurdity. Rather, God in the Bible is revealed as engaging creation (in particular) and humanity in a relationship of love and response that honors human freedom to choose. The application of omniscience to an event-oriented creation need not reach beyond the present. It is God's power and promise-keeping nature that ensures God's word for the world to come.

For instance, consider the thoughts of God in contrast to his inaction in Jeremiah. God's thoughts—or imagination—seek to work good for Judah. However, the LORD will not act to rescue Judah from Babylon because Judah has violated their relationship with God.

> [11] *For I know the thoughts that I think toward you, saith the LORD, thoughts of peace, and not of evil, to give you an expected end.*
>
> JER 29:11

The hope pieces of the prophets are indicative of God's imagination desiring a time when humanity's response to God will be a loving relationship of trust, when the meaning of *shema* (hear and obey) is done willingly. The hope pieces are the divine imagination's refusal to allow the world to perish. Redemption is an event-oriented work, and the defining event is the cross. Moment by moment the sufferance of God allows for an erring creation to continue. Jesus' words on the end indicate openness for a decision on God's part, for a time that is not yet determined.

> [36] *But about that day and hour no one knows, neither the angels of heaven, nor the Son, but only the Father.*
>
> MATT 24:36

Paul affirms in Colossians that the existence of Christ in God precedes all things. I understand this to include the ideas that form the creation. This being said, the ideas that form creation are born of God's imagination.

> [17] *He himself is before all things, and in him all things hold together.*
>
> COL 1:17

Reading Twenty-Nine

The Crucified God-Man

The Divine Dance

Theology is like possibility dancing with impossibility.
It is like an endless wall covered with dialectical writing and God on the other side.
It is the loving embrace of creature and creator, held in the tension of difference.
It is a glorious exercise!

The God-Man

God on a Cross: in Presence and Absence

The cross is the most important revelatory act of God ever accomplished. Contemplation on its meaning is paramount for a Christian. Although the revelation contained in the message of the cross is dependent upon God's creative activity, it supersedes the creative event, not as chronological moment, but as qualitative event. This is so because the message of the cross is an existential, ontological revelation. This means God experiences the cross as an unprecedented, one-time event—an event that reveals God in the most complete manner possible for the sake of humanity. Of course the meaning of the death of Jesus is completed because of his resurrection. That is, the meaning of the cross is viewed through the lens of the resurrection.

> [18] *For the message about the cross is foolishness to those who are perishing, but to us who are being saved it is the power of God.*
>
> 1 Cor 1:18

The cross is not God's invention; God's imagination is not responsible for an object that involves the torture and killing of a human being. The presence of the cross in the revelation of God falls entirely upon the workings of humanity. The cross, like death, is initially foreign to God's experience. Death is God's severest judgment, a judgment that cannot be inflicted upon God because God is self-sustaining life. So, God's son, who is human without exception, can experience death and annul the power of death. The cross is (representative of) humanity's severest judgment—a tortuous and humiliating death.

> [22] *When someone is convicted of a crime punishable by death and is executed, and you hang him on a tree,*
>
> DEUT 21:22

Jesus dies; it is human to die. Death defines the human experience of reality through our inescapable mortality of which we are reminded daily in multitudinous ways. Jesus' death marks God's solidarity with humanity. Our suffering becomes God's suffering, not merely as empathic observer, but as conjoined partner. God's judgment (death) has become his enemy to be destroyed. The death experienced by God on the cross is marked by temporality because of the resurrection.

> [14] *This was now the third time that Jesus appeared to the disciples after he was raised from the dead.*
>
> JOHN 21:14

The revelation of God is intermingled with the revelation of humanity. In order for God to reveal God's self, he must communicate through the linguistic, symbolic, cultural, psychological social world of human existence. God cannot communicate his person directly, but must work through human or creaturely means. For this reason, the teaching of the incarnation is essential for establishing God's desire to communicate himself in relation to human beings. The question, "Who is God?" is answerable only in relation to the questioner. That God's desired relation to humanity springs from God's being (God is love) can only be affirmed by works of love.

Because God enters the creation as a lover longing to be understood, God in effect is viewed through the limitations of the creature's ability to perceive reality. Since the creature does not know God, his / her perception

The Crucified God-Man

is marred. So, God's revelation must be an ongoing effort accomplished through creation, history, promises, and works of love. Because God's self-revelation is played out on the stage of human history, every act of God reveals truth about both God and humanity. When understood, God's revelation exposes humanity's distance from the nature of God (God's holiness).

> Man, (humanity) is not sufficiently God like, but violent, living in a way that is not harmonious with their creator's character, nature, and holiness.

Now we can apply this to the revelation of God on a cross. God's love—and the clarity of who God is—is made clear by the cross in correlation with the question, "Who is man?" Man, (humanity) is the object of God's compelling desire: love. Man, (humanity) is not sufficiently godlike, but violent, living in a way that is not harmonious with their creator's holy character and nature.

I intend to explore both aspects of the cross: as revelation of God and as revelation of man. Then I will explore the cross as the corporate work of God and man in the Lord Jesus Christ.

The Cross: God Revealed

On the cross, God is both present and absent. In the God-Man, through the Incarnation, God is present. Yet, God is more than the human life that is, in essence, God's self. God remains the omnific Father, while stripping himself of all that it means to be God, except that which can be revealed through the Son of God, Jesus. The concept of God's absence is a message of the prophets. The absence of God is communicated in metaphors of human suffering.

> [12] *Therefore I am like maggots to Ephraim, and like rottenness to the house of Judah.*
>
> Hos 5:12

> [15] *I will return again to my place until they acknowledge their guilt and seek my face. In their distress they will beg my favor:*
>
> Hos 5:15

Jesus' experience of the absence of God on the cross makes the cross a work of humanity and not the project of God. However, the paradox of incarnation places God on the cross. The cross exposes humanity's acts of violence as efforts to silence the voice of God. The cross, in effect, is the murder of God by humanity.

Yet, the cross is the work of God; it is the surrender of God into human hands. The cross reveals God's powerlessness to display who he is independent of joining creation and making the human experience his own, permanently. Further, God's love compels him to endure the suffering of a torturous death, in order to draw a clear distinction on the dramatic separation between God and man. The cross reveals that death and violence belong to the way of humanity and are foreign to the way of God. In the light of a benevolent God that refuses to allow the way of man to endure, the cross is an intelligible act of self-revelation, and death is a just judgment.

The cross is God's giving of himself to humanity. It is a picture of God's sense of suffering, matched by God's love. It is God's expression of culpability for the existence of creatures (humanity) that refuse to view death as an acceptable reality, because they bear likeness to God that endows them with sentience, insight, and godlikeness. God's culpability displayed on the cross is not a legal response; it is expressive of God's love and spoken promises. Nor is the culpability of God an admission of guilt; rather, it is love's willingness to endure suffering in order to redeem the creature, in order to demonstrate that God will give more of God's self that humanity might be able to live according to his ways. That God gives more of God's self is revealing of the tension between God and humanity. God creates humanity in need of both Torah (teaching) and relationship with himself (giving of the Spirit). God's giving of himself is the drama of salvation history.

The absence of the Father experienced by Jesus on the cross is the reality of death in relation to God. Because God has embraced humanity and become a particular human being, the defeat of death or mortality is accomplished by Jesus' faith in God's love for humanity. Faith is the relational conduit between man and Holy Spirit. The ongoing maturation of a human being is dependent upon faith.

The presence of God on the cross is representative of the extent to which God's instruction engages reality. God's engagement with human reality gives him a view of existence from the human perspective—a perspective that is redeemed in the life of Jesus, enabling us to see God in the world and yet separate him from creation and evil. God is not the cosmos, but the creator of the cosmos. God is good, whereas evil is a product of God's willingness to suffer the creature's rejection of him, in order that the creature might be redeemed. The existence of the creature in relation to the cosmos is dynamic; meaning, the cosmos, like God, suffers the rejection of God by man.

The Crucified God-Man

> [4] *What are human beings that you are mindful of them,*
> *mortals that you care for them?*
>
> Psalm 8:4

The Cross: Man Revealed

The cross reveals man to be a practitioner of injustice, cruelty, and domination, specifically via systems of culture, politics, and religion. The cross declares the victim innocent. The cross condemns ways of living that do not reject all forms of violence. The cross exposes humanity's inability to live as spirit.

That the God-Man is on the cross—the one that is human without exception, yet God incarnate—reveals the capacity of humanity to be filled with the Spirit of God, live in the way of God, and communicate truth. That the man on the cross is the promised king indicates the calling of Israel has been embodied in the life of this one man. In the cross, humanity's cry for justice is overtaken by God's giving of self in an act of sacrificial love. Love is irrational and self-sacrificial. God's irrational act of love is Jesus on the cross.

The Cross: God and Humanity Reconciled

> [4] *for whatever is born of God conquers the world. And this is the victory that conquers the world, our faith.*
>
> 1 John 5:4

The world is conquered by faith in the God-Man who died upon a cross. The world is the land of exile where surrender to the god of violence is deemed humanity's inevitable service. That God's redemption of humanity was accomplished without the use of violence, or resistance to humanity's violence, opens the eyes of faith to a world without violence to see a nonviolent God and a nonviolent Man.

> [19] *in Christ God was reconciling the world to himself, not counting their trespasses against them, and entrusting the message of reconciliation to us.*
>
> 2 Cor 5:19

Everyday Thoughts

The difference between God and humanity has been embraced into the being of God. The difference is now reconciled in such a way that God's nature can be shared with humanity through the Christ, yet the difference is maintained because Christ is the God-Man and has ascended to equality with God.

> [1] *The LORD says to my lord, "Sit at my right hand until I make your enemies your footstool."*
>
> PSALM 110:1

On a cross God revealed his self through an effort worthy of, and accomplishable only by, a being whose existence is self-sustaining and whose works are creating and redeeming love. This act of self-giving love, in all its sacrificial beauty, draws humanity into the Divine nature (God's holiness), into the being of God. In the God-Man, humanity participates in the salvific act, and sin's history can be healed, forgiveness received, and a new history begun. The death of the God-Man requires a new creation, a resurrection, the revealing of the children of God. This is so because the God-Man is the embracing of the creature into the being of God. The God-Man's life reveals God, exposes humanity, and reconciles the creature with the Creator in a unity of existence that is compatible with the glory (the way) and the holiness (the nature) of God.

> The God-Man's life reveals God, exposes humanity, and reconciles the creature with the creator in a unity of existence that is compatible with the glory (the way) and the holiness (the nature) of God.

> [10] *and in the place where it was said to them, "You are not my people," it shall be said to them, "Children of the living God."*
>
> HOSEA 1:10

Because of the life, death and resurrection of Jesus, a new humanity is born of the old. Human history can be reversed, the damage of sin healed, and there can be a new beginning in a new world, a world where God's presence is ever holding humanity in a divine relationship of self-giving love.

Reading Thirty

An Intertextual Theology from Genesis and Job on the Human Condition

Thoughts for the Irreverent

Have you ever wondered if God made a mistake?
Did God birth this world where hate, violence, and oppression reign freely?
Is God like us, entertained by the sadistic viewing of suffering?
Is God like us, pleasure-seeking at the expense of all those around us?
If it were not for the message of the cross, I think I would become an irreverent speaker like Job,
mad at a god I see and so often unable to see the God of my search in the land of wandering

Competing Stories

I will propose that one of the many theological contributions of the book of Job is to offer a competing narrative to the Genesis story in relation to the ousting of Adam and Eve from the garden and the subsequent murder of Abel by his brother Cain. Further, I will establish that the Joban view on the human condition is an important contrasting story for considering the meaning of Genesis 1–4.

> [7] *Are you the firstborn of the human race? Were you brought forth before the hills?*
>
> JOB 15:7

Everyday Thoughts

This piece of the Joban dialogues is spoken by Eliphaz, who parodies Psalm 8:4 in verse 14 of his argument against Job. The book of Job is theologically rooted in the Old Testament and wrestles with accepted teaching and theology from the perspective of Job the righteous sufferer.

Prior to Eliphaz's assertive accusation that Job is making himself an Adamic archetype while putting his own self forth as the personification of wisdom (Job 15:7), Job declares he will not hide (Job 13:20) and accuses God of hiding (Job 13:24) and treating Job like his enemy. The hiding motif is present in Genesis: Adam hides and God searches for him; this is not Job's experience. Interestingly, the writer of Job does not focus on the eating of the fruit, but on the hiding.

> *8 They heard the sound of the LORD God walking in the garden at the time of the evening breeze, and the man and his wife hid themselves from the presence of the LORD God among the trees of the garden.*
>
> Gen 3:8

In this manner, Job considers himself to be superior to the Adam who hid himself from the paternal God who sought him and clothed him in a garden. Job's God is not a paternal figure who clothes Job, but an almighty nature God who tests Job with suffering. Job trusts his own voice, his own sense of righteousness over the God whom he cannot separate from creation. Job holds God accountable for reality because there is no one else to hold accountable (in the dialogues, Job has no adversary to blame).

We are all guilty of hiding ourselves from one another (the subconscious never lies). We often hide ourselves from God and blame our sins on some other power other than our own. To come before God completely exposed in humility and in all our need is not (for most) a regular practice. We hide behind repentance with a heart unchanged.

The book of Hebrews also focuses on the hiding motif, rather than the eating of the fruit. This focus on hiding is significant and requires that interpreters of the Garden story likewise note that Adam's attempt at hiding is a further reflection on the human condition.

> *13 And before him no creature is hidden, but all are naked and laid bare to the eyes of the one to whom we must render an account.*
>
> Heb 4:13

An Intertextual Theology on the Human Condition

At this point I want to address the human condition as revealed in Genesis 1–4, in contrast to the human condition represented in Job. I will return to additional intertextual connections between the two texts afterwards.

The protohistorical myth of the garden is instructive for understanding the human condition; it is an effort to provide a study at the beginning of humanity that can connect with the human experience. This is the purpose of myth: to present a timeless event that is part of the present reality. We have all been innocent, experiencing life like a garden, only to discover another voice that draws us toward understanding the good and evil that is in the world. The garden story insists that the consciousness of humanity was a creative act of God upon forming the first male and female from the ground. The tree is not in possession of a magical fruit; rather, it is the prohibition that is the line of demarcation. The prohibition is representative of the voice of God that is qualitatively different than the creature (the human beings). The human beings' natural proclivity is to understand the world in which they live. God is absent from their life, they are together alone in the garden, unlike the beasts, and possessing likeness with their Creator. God's absence seems to be as purposeful as the prohibition, it beckons the first pair to seek to survive on their own, to access knowledge, both good and evil. In their innocence, they cannot even conceive what constitutes good and evil.

Eve is depicted as standing at the moment of choice: the fruit is aesthetically pleasing to the eye, ethically it is good for food, and religiously it provides insight into the world. Eve demonstrates inquisitive intelligence and Adam is present with her. Together they experience their ongoing growth as conscious beings, and discover that living independently of God's voice is their ontological completion. They are of the ground, part of the creation. They cannot remain innocent spirits; they are flesh.

The serpent is the voice of Eve's inner dialogue. I think the serpent also represents the chaos in creation, which is first depicted in primeval waters. That the serpent is a symbol worn upon the headdress of Egypt's pharaohs may be indicative of humanity's step towards self-deification, at least for a few that govern the rest. The serpent as a beast cannot talk; it is Eve's imagination that has projected a conversation with the wild aspect of creation.

In God's absence, human beings begin their journey of life, their pristine beginning is unmanageable, and their completion requires separation from their Creator (who has left them alone). God's voice is not (entirely) compatible with their reality; some form of reconciliation between humanity and God is required and is not yet accomplished. Their mortality is their journey; it is their natural state for which they were created. To be human is to die. So Jesus must also experience death.

Death is God's decision or, if you will, God's judgment. Humanity cannot live indefinitely apart from God. If my reader is aware that I have not used the word sin, neither has the writer of Genesis. The word sin does not appear in the text until Genesis 4:7 when God is speaking with Cain. However, in light of the New Testament we can say sin entered the world with Adam and Eve's consciousness of their status as creatures apart from God. Along with this concept of sin as separation, as inability to reconcile God's voice with reality, as part of the human condition, it does not keep humanity from being able to choose the good; as God so clearly states to Cain.

> [7] *If you do well, will you not be accepted? And if you do not do well, sin is lurking at the door; its desire is for you, but you must master it."*
>
> GEN 4:7

The creation of humanity is not complete without God's absence, without the need for human beings to leave their innocence, to begin the journey of life from birth to death. However, that God returns to instruct and clothe his newly created human beings indicates God has not left humanity without hope for a reunion of grander measure. This singular act portrays God as entering human history, a history which can only begin after the act of separation, after death is recognized, after awareness of self that uncovers nakedness, exposes the inner thoughts of human beings. We have been set free by the anxiety of choice to fulfill the task of learning to live.

> I think life is a 'crash course' on the distance between God and creature, so that in eternity we will be accepting of our adoption as children of God with the humility displayed in Christ Jesus.

I think life is a crash course on the distance between God and creature, so that in eternity we will be accepting of our adoption as children of God with the humility displayed in Christ Jesus. Perhaps the book of Qohelet (Ecclesiastes) can be understood in this light, the seeming vanity (*hevel*) of life is weighed against the sense of eternity in our hearts that calls us to rise above, to become flesh and spirit.

When the word sin makes its appearance in Genesis 4, it is displayed as an insatiable desire to be more than one's brother, a desire uncontrolled that erupts into murder. The speechless Abel is victim to his brother's sin. The righteous Abel's blood (life) cries out from the ground and God hears.

An Intertextual Theology on the Human Condition

From the beginning, God hears the voice of innocent sufferers and forgives their murderers, allowing them to live, giving them opportunity to choose another way—the way of God, the way of peace, of life.

The sexual awareness that accompanies life and death enters the world with the completion of Adam and Eve's self-consciousness. This is indicated in their sense of nakedness; the hiding is indicative of much more. Existentially, we human beings suffer from incompleteness; we are finite mortals bearing the image of God, possessing God's likeness, while being creatures that enter time with a beginning moving towards an end outside of the garden of God—the place where life erupts from the ground at his bequest, even at the intimacy of his hands.

As gendered beings, sexuality is normal, good, and to be exercised under an agreement of promise, a covenant. Whereas hiding is our self-conscious effort to keep our anxiety over choice covered, rather than expose ourselves as incomplete, as works in progress. Love does not come without a promise, and a promise must be confirmed with a covenant. It is in the marriage relationship that the male and female can overcome their hiding from one another and develop the possibility of learning to stand naked before God (like Job).

So, how does the prohibition not to eat from the tree contribute to our self-understanding of the human condition? It is representative of the realm between faith and the visible, between flesh and spirit. The prohibition is a warning that humanity can trespass too far into the realm of knowledge and produce evil. We human beings reach for more than we should, we do not restrain ourselves. Perhaps this is most apparent in the production of nuclear weapons. Like Cain, we must learn to choose the good, to reject the violence that makes some perpetrators and others victims. The compromise of life for scientific gain is evil.

The failure to view the garden story as instructive on the human condition—as a myth with limits—results in views that promote the idea that Adam and Eve were complete prior to the entrance of the anxiety of choice. The presence of the tree with its prohibition introduces the anxiety as an external object, an opportunity for making a choice. The inwardness of the first human beings was brought to life through an inevitable choice, to choose to live and pursue knowledge because God is absent, yet present through the creation that is conducive to life. The clothing of the first male and female indicates their superiority to the animals and the care of God to provide for humanity sufficiently for their flourishing in creation. The sword at the entrance to the garden is both warning and inviting, for while it cuts deeply into the soul and exposes our nakedness, our shame, our need to become, the sword also represents the word of God, a word that will become flesh. History must become reconciled with God; it is foreign to God. Humanity is like God, but flesh. God must reconcile humanity also, and so ensues the drama of salvation, the story of God and humanity.

The book of Job as a theological work on the human condition begins east of Eden and with a myth (the prologue). Job's story does not begin in a garden, but the flourishing life of a wealthy sheik, whose experience of life is complete. The antagonist is not a serpent but a satan (*hasatan*); not an inner voice, but a member of the mythical heavenly council. The man is not an inheritor of some hereditary sin; he is whole and upright, a man of integrity. He is the finest example of humanity that God has ever seen. Nonetheless, he must be tested. Life cannot be lived free from suffering, free from the accusatory voice of creation that inhibits humanity from living without struggle. As a character, Job resists any concept of inherited sin that posits total depravity in humanity.

Job is a voice for humanity; he has had the best of life. Job has experienced great affluence and yet been responsible to his fellow human beings. In a whirlwind of war and catastrophe, he experiences loss of family, servants, and wealth. In a few more lines, his health is stricken with severe calamity and his wife betrays him with an invitation to curse (bless) God and die. Life becomes a torturous experience, and Job laments the day of his birth like a victim of torture who refuses to die. So begin the dialogues where we leave the mythical world of a heavenly scene and join the world of the living, where suffering is inescapable.

The dialogues of the book of Job are an honest man's relentless complaint and insights into the human condition. His tenacity to hold onto God is exemplary; he does so by blaming God for his plight. Job is a story that places blame for the human condition on God. Adam did as much when he told God he ate the fruit because of the woman whom God gave him. I take this statement to be humorous, for only if Adam existed alone could he be free from the reality of the human condition and live without anxiety. Yet it was not good for him to be alone in the eyes of God. Without the woman, without gender, procreation, and death, there could be no history, no salvation, no humanity.

Adam hides from God because he is afraid and ashamed. Job requests God to relieve him of the fear and dread endemic to God's presence. Job declares that he will not hide himself but appear boldly and wear any accusation against him as winner's scarf across his chest. The book of Job is written prior to the revelation of God in Christ and has some limitations on an accurate portrayal of God. Still, God watches Job, is happy about Job's goodness (integrity), and must not let Job escape suffering. The book of Job as a portrayal of the human condition voices innocence from every aspect of human experience. There are good people in the world; we are not all totally depraved. Depravity is not biologically inherited.

The sins of the fathers are the repercussions of their lives, their teaching, their sociocultural constructs that we accept without questioning. We experience the world they created; we can stop and wait for the God who clothes Adam and Eve, the God who meets Job and does not explain himself, the God who has now revealed (and exposed) his self in his son Jesus Christ, and we can form a different reality. Jesus called it the kingdom of God; John called it eternal life; Luke called it the Way; Paul called it being in Christ; the writer of Hebrews called it rest.

It is human to be born, to die, suffer, experience betrayal, anxiety, loss, catastrophe, and be able to choose to do good in the midst of all our struggles. Jesus experienced the human condition and was a righteous sufferer, an innocent victim. Jesus is our model. The human condition is not paradise; we are east of Eden. Eden is a dream, a hope, not a return to innocence, but reconciliation with God as God reconciles God's self to humanity over the course of history.

Reading Thirty-One

Don't Blame the Serpent

"I have Solved the Problem of Evil," Said No One Ever

Evil Exists
How long O Lord
I am Silent
Until Suffering Overwhelms
Then I am Silent
Hammered to the Earth
With You O Lord I will Rise Again

No Devil but Self-Will

There are forces in reality that press human beings into behaving and acting in ways that indicate our freedom for good is obstructed and we cannot escape the ensuing tragedies that mark us as unable to live in accordance with the goodness of God. Over time we named this force, gave this force an image, developed a history of existence for this force, and exalted this force to near equality with God. Our only good response is the love that endures suffering with hope.

We failed to note that the absence of God left us as prey to ourselves. Our need for God far outweighs our parasitical nemesis. Unable to live in harmony with the Spirit of the one God, we gave birth to another and multiplied that one mythological deity of evil with an army of demons. Because we experienced evil as greater than us, we would not accept our accountability for its existence, nor could we place its origin on our conception of a good or holy God. Somewhere in the recesses of the human psyche lay this affirmation, a mark of the Creator—an ultimate good, free from evil.

Flailing in chaos, living out of control, unable to halt the brevity of life, the harshness of disease, the inevitability of disruptive disaster, life became sacrificial. In order that some might survive and advance beyond others, large segments of humanity were sacrificed to the structural injustices of kings and conquerors. The pursuit for power, to avoid working the ground, to avoid smallness, resulted in some choosing to use the force of evil. So violence became an accepted norm, an inevitable reality, the god of the warrior, the friend of the inventor of money, the sacrificial ritual for cleansing an evolutionary process, as elites sought to unlock mysteries and gain eternal life.

What madness possessed humanity to think that the pursuit of Paradise, the desire for peace, the hope to live forever, could be attained by human will and abuse of the creation? I suspect the Hebrews began to understand violence as an inexcusable evil when they listed it as the cause for the annihilation of humanity in their mythological flood story (Gen 6). So, their God of peace placed his bow upside down in the sky, in order to indicate that God is not at war with humanity; God is not violent.

Am I free? Am I a puppet? Am I a victim? Or am I all these at once? I refuse to be a puppet; I reject that anyone should be a victim; I am only left with freedom. I am free to be human, to be all that our Creator, our Father, intends for us to be. What will it mean to be free in a world where so many are not? Are they not puppets of evil and victims of violence? I am free to think, speak, write, and live in contrast to the precepts of culturally accepted norms that inhibit my voice. What does this freedom mean in a world where darkness prevails and the good is unrecognizable, where death turns humanity into beasts?

I am older now, my strength has failed, my story is more behind than ahead of me. I must breathe in the life eternal that springs forth from my Creator, my Father, my God. I struggle at the threshold of an absolute rejection of violence, but such a time is beyond the violence of death that permeates our existence. How then to live with this violence inside of me, this survival mechanism that insists on the right of all human beings to live unmolested by the violence inflicted by the powers of greed, by the violent who govern the earth with injustice?

I have walked streets where young women are sold or rented, bearing a number on their body so they could be identified by the prospective buyer. I thought of stringing wire to trip sex tourists. I thought of placing sand in the generators that serviced their bars so that when the power went out their business stopped. I had many other thoughts. Perhaps there is a time for such activity? However, the problem with violence is that it escalates to a place of horror before it wanes to erupt again.

I am sure the answer lies in walking the way of Jesus.

Yes, laws help. Yet I understand the nature of law. One law requires an infinite amount of laws to cover every possibility; there is no end to the writing of laws. Surely God has given us law because we would not live according to his voice that walks the paths of paradise.

Where is he who is good? How can I find him? I see his power displayed in the cosmos, his wisdom sewn into the creation, even his testimony written in the moral conscience of the innocent. The cosmos sings of his existence, the structures of life to his wisdom, the innocent to this goodness.

> Surely God has given us law because we would not live according to his voice that walks the paths of paradise.

If I seek to know him will he reveal himself to me? Has he revealed himself to all humanity? If he did, surely death's end would be present with his appearing. So, the resurrection is the sign of God's presence, but the cross is God's ultimate revelation of his person. Freedom then is to refuse violence and accept being a victim as one that does not allow the powers to see you as a victim but as a threat to their order.

The metaphor of God as a lion is a picture of how humanity perceives God in absence, in the severity of the judgment of death. However, the picture of God as a lamb represents presence and absolute solidarity with humanity.

It is a sad reality that so many fail to anchor evil in the failure of humanity to become spirit—to be fully human, like Jesus. It is not political power or influence that will change the world for the better, but people who become spirit, as Jesus did. Human beings were not created to rule over one another; we are not fit to rule over one another. We were created to serve one another in love, to be our brother's keeper.

> Human beings were not created to rule over one another; we are not fit to rule over one another.

In the present age, the greatest evil on the face of the earth is the poverty that reduces the majority of humanity to victims of progress. This evil lies at the feet of the industrialized nations, the first nations to benefit from scientific advance and technological progress.

I am convinced that there is no greater indication of spiritual maturation than a commitment to nonviolence and serving the poor. It is praxis that informs our reflection on the word, and praxis is to replicate the life of Jesus in our distinctly different human life. The subversive power of goodness can bring change to the world.

I want to be free, free enough to live like Jesus. I have a dream; God help me.

Reading Thirty-Two

Sexuality, Temporality, and Gender

Spirituality and Human Sexuality

The spiritual aspect of human sexuality is not in relation to God. Rather, the spiritual aspect of sexuality is in relation to the violation of the natural structures of creation. It is the spiritual aspect of sexuality that negates the good, because it mars the creation and reduces sexuality to instinct rather than insight; instinct is to cast off restraint and respond only to desire. This being said, it is also true that the spiritual aspect of human sexuality is in relation to the good structures of creation put in place by God, however, not in direct relation to God's Spirit.

God is not a sexual being, sexuality is foreign to God's being and experience; it belongs to the creature. Jesus' celibacy indicates that engaging in sex does not contribute to the fulfilling of the image of God. Jesus will conclude that sexuality does not survive the resurrection, although gender distinctiveness will. To abuse sexual life is to participate in uncreation, which is the arena of the demonic. Sexuality belongs to the sphere of the sacred between a male and a female.

The spirituality of marriage is in the promise, the relationship, not the sexual act. God is not involved, does not participate, and does not violate the sphere of the sacred between a male and a female. Human sexuality is love and worship of the other, not love and worship of God. This is portrayed in the Song of Solomon, a book that celebrates male and female sexuality. The absence of God in the Song of Solomon is confirming of human sexuality as sacred apart from God. The error of Israel's neighbors was to attribute spirituality to sexuality.

Becoming Spirit

That God is spirit is the communicative reality about the being and person of God, which remains invisible for us human beings. Of course that God is spirit seems to be the essential reflection of omnific attributes in a finite creation. A God that is present everywhere and possesses all power and knowledge must be invisible in relation to the creation, or the creation could not exist. The creation is not God but is separate from the being and person of God. Nonetheless, the creation displays God's omnific self. The creation must exist within the being of God and be sustained by God (at least initially with a burst of power), while not being God. Yet, God's person can only be revealed through relationship with the creature. This is basic to God's self-revelation in Exodus 34:5–7.

We must use metaphor to talk about spirit, so the Spirit of God is like an invisible, unpredictable, uncontrollable wind. The origin of the human form is found in the imagination of God. Some theologians suggest the possibility that the human form is derived from some distinct reality about the centralized presence of God. Such a thought is built upon the theophanic appearances of God in the Old Testament. I understand these theophanic appearances to be forerunners of the incarnation. The appearance of God in human form suggests the possibility of God taking humanity into God's self, the deification of humanity. However, God remains one and the creature remains creature.

An omnific being can share his/her self but not produce offspring of an identical being; there is only one God. So, God is a genderless being, a Spirit. For this reason, sexuality is foreign to the being and person of God. We might suggest that since God has become flesh and lived among us that God chose a gender and therefore now possesses gender. It is evident that God had to choose to become either a male or a female. I suggest that God could have done either and fulfilled the revelation of God in Christ Jesus. However, Jesus states that in our coming life with God, beyond death and the grave, marriage is no longer a part of human reality. I do not think we have to abolish the specifics of gender. Like Augustine, I understand that resurrection must keep that which is distinctive of the person. Of course, there are unanswered or unanswerable questions here relating to our genitals and biological functions. So John states clearly:

> ² Beloved, we are God's children now; what we will be has not yet been revealed. What we do know is this: when he is revealed, we will be like him, for we will see him as he is
>
> 1 JOHN 3:2

It is certain that both male and female are created in the image and likeness of God. So, the sustaining of some distinctive traits as male and female does not in any way hinder our existence as God's (created) children. The absence of marriage in the resurrection seems to indicate a loss of procreation and of sexuality. Since sexuality is foreign to God, it is fitting that his children no longer marry or procreate. This seems to be Jesus' conclusion.

Sexuality is a problem because it functions through instinctual desires and this is the very source of its attraction, the challenge to become spirit does not exist when engaging in sexual activity, because sexuality is foreign to God. However, becoming flesh and living a human life is not foreign to God. The celibacy of Jesus on this count alone is significant. The last Adam, Jesus, enters humanity through the same means as other human beings, but does not continue humanity by the same means.

> ⁸ Bear fruits worthy of repentance. Do not begin to say to yourselves, "We have Abraham as our ancestor"; for I tell you, God is able from these stones to raise up children to Abraham.
>
> LUKE 3:8

However, humanity has consistently deified sexuality as a form of worship to excite their (imagined) gods, or the spirits of the cosmos. In effect, humanity created imaginary gods in their image, sexual beings of desire and violence.

In the Bible, the marriage metaphor serves to communicate the relationship of God and humanity. Human sexuality becomes oneness of spirit between covenant-keeping male and female persons, each sharing in one another. We are creatures and our sexuality is to be restricted to a covenant relationship of commitment, love, and, if possible, procreation. It is not good that the male or the female be alone. It is through this metaphor that sexuality is sanctified, not as the act itself, nor as something that God participates in via spirit, but as creatures fulfilling the desire of God for a growing field of humanity—creatures born of relationships reflective of

God's self, reflective in promise-keeping (covenant), in love, and participating (with the help of God) in creating.

The abuse of sexuality is to participate in the demonic and reduce the sanctifying element of sexuality to raw instinct. All insight is lost, and the image-bearing human beings become beasts. The spiritual aspect of human sexuality is in relation to the good structures of creation put in place by God and not in direct relation to God's Spirit. Human sexuality is a celebration of life between the male and female, where the image of God in promise-keeping, love, and the possibility of creating (procreation) is present. This is not to annul sexual life when procreation is no longer possible (the lesson of Sarah); the Song of Solomon placed in the canon as a celebration of human sexuality attests to the joy of sexual love as part of the human experience.

Sexuality carries with it a sense of innocence, a return to the nakedness of the garden. At the same time, it is a practice that carries with it caution and taboo. Noah should have not engaged in drunkenness and sexuality, he should have ensured that his tent door was secured (Gen 9:20–29). Human sexuality carries with it a sense of the sacred; it is sacredness between a man and a woman, as creatures under the blessing of God.

Of course, sexuality is one of our biggest problems. Uncontrolled sexual desire tears at the structures of reality that form healthy human lives and families. We attempt to retain a certain distinctiveness between the sexes through dress, hair styles, make up, and behaviors.

I will take a lighter tone now with this piece of writing. I have often wondered why sexual desire has to be so strong, just as I have wondered why pain has to be so intensely painful. I am sure God wants humanity to live, flourish, multiply, and fill the earth. This implies that the earth isn't actually filled. All one has to do is fly overhead and observe the vast amounts of unpopulated land mass. Instead, we have concentrated populations in cities and on our coastlines. The poor multiply (like the slaves in Egypt), in spite of their affliction. In spite of war and calamities, human beings continue to populate.

Our desire for the other—for love and sex—drives us to populate. This being said, only an educated and informed people filled with the Spirit can restrain the sexual desire of humanity within the structures of creation's order.

There are other problems, such as the right of women to bear children, whether they are attractive or not, whether they can find a husband or not. East of Eden, regulating human behavior is a real problem.

Reading Thirty-Three

Jacob's Dream

Genesis 28:10–22

Awakening Consciousness
Immaturity of Mind
A Dreamer
A Head is not made for Stone
Awake O'Sleeper and Christ shall give you Light
There is no Stairway to Heaven
God Speaks
A Man of Peace and Wisdom is Born

Dreaming

Young Jacob departs with haste to escape the rage of his brother. He will leave the comfort of living in tents to sleep in the wilderness, with a stone to lay his head upon. This is a strange thing: a man using a stone for a pillow. It is even stranger that the stone would be assigned sacred status for its role in Jacob's encounter with the presence and promise of Yahweh. It is through a dream of heavenly messengers using a stone staircase for their journeying from the realm of God to the realm of man that Jacob hears the affirming of a promise by Yahweh—a promise that is not unfamiliar to Jacob, for it is at the heart of his fathers' faith.

> Man's head was not made to lie upon stones any more than a stone can become the house of God.

The thoughts of Jacob on his journey are not given to us in a narrator's commentary, but revealed to us through a dream. In a land filled with stones, Jacob longs for a word from God to bring him some hope. A dream of a stone staircase for heavenly messengers is reflective of Jacob's longing to hear from the God who spoke with his fathers. That Jacob's exhaustion, both physical and emotional, is matched by the discomfort of the stone that he lays his head upon is instructive. This is so because Jacob will have to learn to use his intelligence to flourish in the home of his relatives. God will be with Jacob by blessing his intelligence, his understanding of the world. Man's head was not made to lie upon stones any more than a stone can become the house of God.

While dreaming, Yahweh stands beside Jacob and affirms the promise given to his grandfather and father—a promise that will be carried by Jacob as well. Jacob's longing for a word from God is revealed in his dream of heavenly messengers; however, it is Yahweh who speaks to Jacob and not a messenger. Yahweh's promise includes going and remaining with Jacob during his sojourn. Further, Yahweh promises to bring Jacob back from his exile.

When Jacob is fully awake, he understands his experience to be both dream and encounter with the reality of Yahweh's word and presence. Alone, Jacob commemorates the experience with a ceremony and anoints the rock on which he laid his head. Jacob knows that God is to be with him on his sojourn and is not bound to the place he is commemorating. Yahweh has told him that he would be with him and keep him wherever he goes, and bring him back to the land of his father.

Jacob will not be looking to heavenly beings to rescue or speak to him. Jacob's revelation of Yahweh is affirming of monotheistic understanding. Yahweh has made the world and the minds of men that dream. Yahweh interprets our dreams; Jacob's dream was representative of his longing to receive a message from God. Yahweh's promises are sure, Yahweh is with Jacob in diverse ways, and freedom from superstition is one of Yahweh's revelations to Jacob.

The house of God is the human being who hears the word of Yahweh, and the gate of heaven is the human mind where God's words are understood. Jacob's ceremony is not the rash absurdity of a primitive mind or a foolish boy. It is the careful crafting of a writer of Scripture. The purpose of the ceremony is to establish that although Yahweh is not confined to place, place is important for human beings; and God is attentive to this truth.

Jacob anoints the stone, (representative of his mind) and declares it to be the house of God.

The differentiation between Jacob's dream and Yahweh's appearance and promise is crucial for grasping the progressive teaching on dreams in the book of Genesis. It is this differentiation that enables Jacob to realize he has been blessed with a good mind and if he will use his mind, God will bless him.

> Yahweh is not confined to place, place is important for human beings.

I propose that Jacob's differentiation between superstition (angels ascending and descending) and the appearance of Yahweh speaking reveals to Jacob that God reads the minds of men, even their dreams. God keeps his word and is more expansive (present) than a local or tribal deity. Jacob's experience has connected him with that which differentiates human beings from all other creatures; God is with them in their journey of life and understands the phenomenon of dreaming. The mind is an expression of the heart and God can communicate, make promises, and live relationally with insightful human beings. God hears even our thoughts.

> Jacob's initial awakening as a fully conscious person occurs when his dreaming ceases and he hears God speaking. His test of awakening is the wrestling match with *God, Esau, and Self.*

With this lesson learned, Jacob will succeed in the house of his superstitious father-in-law, Laban. Jacob's awakening has revealed to him the meaning and power of dreams. Further, Jacob understands dreaming as an aesthetic exercise of the mind and uses his educational encounter with Yahweh to play upon the immaturity of Laban.

I propose that Jacob learns the art of breeding animals and in so doing controls the physical appearance of the flocks. Jacob's practice of breeding the animals in front of the rods is a ruse to keep from Laban his knowledge of breeding. Jacob appeals to Laban's superstitious beliefs and lets Laban suppose that the breeding in front of the rods is the cause for Jacob's success.

Granting to Jacob superior breeding skills does not remove the blessing of Yahweh upon the entire enterprise. Yahweh works with Jacob's efforts and blesses them. Laban's superstitious belief is exemplified in the idols he keeps and his pursuit of Jacob to retrieve the idols. The pillar of stones that Jacob sets up as a boundary marker serves two purposes. First, the oath that they will not cross over to do each other harm is instructive; borders are to be respected and crossed over only to aid the other, not to do harm. Second, the differentiation between Jacob's family and Laban's is the difference between monotheism and superstition. Monotheism and superstition are not compatible and bring about separation just as much as Laban's greed and Jacob's hard work and wisdom.

Likewise, the placing of stones in these two stories is related. The stone Jacob anointed is indicative of the presence of Yahweh. The stones Jacob places for a boundary are God entering the world through Jacob's actions for peace. Yahweh is present in the lives of those who seek peace and utilize their insight in relation to humanity, God, and the world, in order to prosper.

Reading Thirty-Four

Land, Peace, and Promises from God

From Dust to Dust
People of the Earth
Land is Gift
Hear the Father of Faith whose sole possession of land was a graveyard
Is not the whole earth before you?
Peace is the sacred space of God's children
Land is not sacred
I will heal your land

Room for Peace

In the Bible, land is an important theological concept. A number of excellent books have been written on the subject. My purpose in this article is to provide a biblical view on how land is to be acquired, nation-states acknowledged, and peace pursued.

I will begin with the life of Abraham as an example for acquiring land under the promise of God. Abraham was an altar-building, well-digging, peacemaking, nomadic herdsman. Abraham traveled throughout the land, building altars. He was not to put a chisel to the stones that comprised the altars. The altars were designed to collapse back into the land without any evidence that they were ever built. The lesson for the reader is that the land is acquired not by human effort, but by relationship with the God that makes room for the family of Abraham. The impermanence of the altars speaks to the effort of men to build religious monuments that are more representative of human attempts at grandeur and control than of God.

Land, Peace, and Promises from God

As the years passed, Abraham remained an alien in a land promised to him and his descendants. The only piece of the land that Abraham ever owned in a legally recognized manner was a graveyard. This is a significant lesson for all of us: the only land we will ever truly own is the piece where we return to the dust from which we were made. Abraham purchased land in the land God said he would give to him and establish his descendants. Perhaps Abraham's purchase of the land was acknowledgment that God gave him the wealth to do so, and so also gave him the land itself. Abraham's purchase from the people of the land sits in contrast to the later military conquests of his descendants.

Abraham deferred to his nephew Lot the better land, while preferring peace and God's blessing. Abraham refused to fight for land, but he did launch a rescue campaign to recover his family from those that would enslave them. Abraham also refused to profit from his campaign, and it is notable that the narrative of Lot's rescue avoids mentioning any violence.

Of course, land is necessary for life. Human beings must have space to move about and must take from the land the richness that God has provided for our use and sustenance. Land is an ongoing part of the biblical narratives. However, the acquisition of land is an ethical matter and it is God who claims ultimate ownership of all the earth. Isaac, like his father, displays another helpful lesson on the acquisition of land for human flourishing.

Although Isaac's father had dug wells in the land, Isaac would not fight to maintain any right to the wells and the land that surrounded them. Isaac moved twice from wells previously dug by his father, because the local inhabitants protested his presence and his right to the water and the land. Abraham had dug two wells and Isaac must dig his own well at a distance from other people groups. Isaac's response upon completing the well without contention testifies to God's work of making room for him in the land. The association of water rights with land ownership is present in this story, as is the need for water.

> [22] *He moved from there and dug another well, and they did not quarrel over it; so he called it Rehoboth, saying, "Now the LORD has made room for us, and we shall be fruitful in the land."*
>
> Gen 26:22

Like his father, Isaac's life is an example of peace and patience. Isaac endured transience and hardship for the sake of peace, rather than fighting for land. Like his father, Isaac dug wells that provided water in a dry land. The well-digging enterprise sits in contrast to developing a class of warriors in his familial clan. These peaceful actions of Isaac culminated in God's presence and in the reaffirmation of the promises given to his father.

The story of Jacob offers a lesson on land, borders, and violence in the human family. Initially Jacob fled his home to avoid being killed by his brother. Esau had good reason to be angry with his twin brother. Jacob could have offered him some stew without demanding the birthright of the firstborn. Jacob and his conniving mother took advantage of an aging Isaac, in order to secure the traditional blessing from father to son.

When Jacob, the expert animal breeder, fled from his father-in-law, he was confronted by Laban along the route of his departure. Violence was near to breaking out between Laban and Jacob's families. Jacob had to leave and return to the land from whence he had come. However, he and Laban set up a boundary, a few stones to mark the spot. They made a promise never to cross this boundary to ever harm one another. This is Scripture's way of teaching us about why borders should be set and how we are to cross over recognized borders. Borders are made to keep peace between people groups and are to be crossed over without intent to harm the people of the land.

> [52] *This heap is a witness, and the pillar is a witness, that I will not pass beyond this heap to you, and you will not pass beyond this heap and this pillar to me, for harm.*
>
> GENESIS 31:52

The tension of this story is in the countercultural elements of Genesis, which challenge accepted practices, such as the right of the firstborn. The entire episode is dramatically enhanced by the fact that Esau and Jacob are twins. The book of Genesis as a whole should be studied with literary attentiveness. Genesis can be read with the following emphases: countercultural text, peacemaking text, female heroines, God as character, a theology of God, a protohistorical document, an historical document, character development, founding myths, and an etiology for numerous realities, including psychology and anthropological phenomena.

It is the countercultural aspect of reading Genesis that reveals to the reader the conflict between later cultural practices that were honored as sacred. The peacemaking practices of the patriarchs are countercultural to the warring of Israel for conquest of the land. Likewise, the book of Exodus presents as God's will that the conquest of the land was to be accomplished in a similar manner to the events of Israel's liberation from Egyptian tyranny. The practice of war was not a part of God's intention for Israel's growth as a people, nor for their reception of land as a gift.

> [27] I will send my terror in front of you, and will throw into confusion all the people against whom you shall come, and I will make all your enemies turn their backs to you. [28] And I will send the pestilence in front of you, which shall drive out the Hivites, the Canaanites, and the Hittites from before you. [29] I will not drive them out from before you in one year, or the land would become desolate and the wild animals would multiply against you. [30] Little by little I will drive them out from before you, until you have increased and possess the land.
>
> EXOD 23:27–30

I want to entertain a few events that depict God's efforts to keep Israel from becoming a warring people. To develop a warring class is an ongoing temptation in society. To maintain a standing army is, in the Scripture, idolatrous. It seems that God cannot keep Israel from warring. However, this does not stop God from aiding Israel. It also makes discerning when God did, or did not, aid Israel, an interpretive task. I will compile some texts and readings for developing a peacemaking theology that rejects war as a God-ordained practice.

The following verse is an interesting part for developing my claim that God does not want Israel to develop a standing army.

> [9] And Joshua did to them as the LORD commanded him; he hamstrung their horses, and burned their chariots with fire.
>
> JOSHUA 11:9

Horses and chariots were the tanks of ancient warfare. The capture of horses and chariots would enhance Israel's war machine with superior weapons for engaging their enemies. Horses that are hamstrung are no longer useful for pulling chariots or for riding as warhorses. Of course, burning the chariots is a complete repudiation of trusting in weapons of war for deliverance from one's enemies. This practice also inhibits the development of a warrior class trained to ride horses and maneuver chariots.

Israel's Kings were Forbidden to Keep Horses and Chariots.

> [16] *Even so, he must not acquire many horses for himself, or return the people to Egypt in order to acquire more horses.*
>
> DEUT 17:16

The prayer that Hosea urged Israel to live out was a repudiation of warfare, trusting in the world's empires for protection, or deifying the architectural accomplishments of city builders, whose gods adorned their edifices.

> [3] *Assyria shall not save us; we will not ride upon horses; we will say no more, "Our God," to the work of our hands. In you the orphan finds mercy.*
>
> HOSEA 14:3

The revelation of God in Christ Jesus upon a cross is the interpretive lens through which all the Scripture must be subjected. When Scripture displays God in any manner conflicting with the revelation of God in Christ, then the problem is not with God, but with our reading. God's struggle is how to reveal himself to human beings. His revelation is intra-historical. It is progressive, yet consistent with God's character and image (holiness). God in the Old Testament is not a god of violence that calls for *cherem*, or the slaughter of entire communities, in war. The narrative interpretations of God's speeches are subject to the revelation of God in Christ. We should not read them as absolute communication of God's will, but as that of a people consumed in the world—a people needing more than Sinai.

I will offer the following passage to demonstrate that Deuteronomy presents the *cherem* as something other than the slaughtering of human beings merciless, genocidal acts.

> [1] *When the LORD your God brings you into the land that you are about to enter and occupy, and he clears away many nations before you—the Hittites, the Girgashites, the Amorites, the Canaanites, the Perizzites, the Hivites, and the Jebusites, seven nations mightier and more numerous than you* [2] *and when the LORD your God gives them over to you and you defeat them, then you must utterly destroy them. Make no covenant with them and show them no mercy.* [3] *Do not intermarry with them, giving your daughters to their sons or taking their daughters for your sons,* [4] *for that would turn away your*

Land, Peace, and Promises from God

children from following me, to serve other gods. Then the anger of the LORD would be kindled against you, and he would destroy you quickly. ⁵ But this is how you must deal with them: break down their altars, smash their pillars, hew down their sacred poles, and burn their idols with fire.

DEUT 7:1–5

There are two parts of this piece that provide for the manner in which a people are to be destroyed. First, they must be assimilated into God's people; their cultural ideologies of life and god must be destroyed. Intermarriage is initially forbidden, but is approved after the people are brought into Israel's covenants with God. Moses views this as a generational process and sets a rule.

⁸ The children of the third generation that are born to them may be admitted to the assembly of the LORD.

DEUT 23:8

Deuteronomy 7:5 is clear that the method for destroying a people is to dismantle their religious symbolic world, and in effect the adhesive elements of their culture that are inconsistent with Israel's covenant God. Other peoples must become subjected to the kingship of God and embrace the covenants; that is, bless themselves by living in peace and harmony with Israel and her God. This living in peace is a mutual affair, and Israel cannot teach other nations the way of peace when she refuses to trust her God, choosing instead to practice war like the other nations. The instructions for annihilation *cherem* in Deuteronomy are not to kill. I think it is clear that the problem with Israel is that they practiced war and killing; in effect, they were like all the peoples around them. Warring requires a warrior class, a king to conscript their children. Such activity is the rejection of Yahweh, the God of the Hebrews, the God of all peoples.

Warring is the philosophy of Plato, the way of the world's alleged wisdom. Any group of people that claim to be Christian cannot practice war. As a people, Christians are citizens of the will of God, that is, of heaven. Like Israel in exile, we are people without a particular land to represent our Lord and us. Yet, in exile we learn to become the people of God. The earth is the Lord's and we wait for his coming that he might make room for us. In the meantime, we are people of peace, and we build altars of living sacrifice

EVERYDAY THOUGHTS

throughout the earth. We dig wells, seeking to bring water to thirsty lands in both physical and spiritual ways. We come in peace, refusing to fight and kill in order to acquire the resources of other peoples. We do not justify the inherent greed that propels capitalistic ventures across the earth in the name of democracy.

The establishment of Israel as a nation-state came about when Israel's kinship tribal groups formed a confederation and later became a nation under the rule of a king. Primarily it is the books of 1 and 2 Samuel that record for us a theological view on the development of the state. David understood his kingdom to be established when he had acquired a city where religious, military, and governmental power could be centralized, and other nation-states could recognize his accomplishment.

> Warring is the philosophy of Plato, the way of the world's alleged wisdom.

[11] *King Hiram of Tyre sent messengers to David, along with cedar trees, and carpenters and masons who built David a house.*

2 SAM 5:11

The following passage from Deuteronomy stops a man from becoming a king by requiring him to become a servant. The ongoing story of the gospel is how God is, and will become, King over all humanity. Nation-states are temporary constructs birthed by God, in order to bring some peace into a world where men choose to live like raiders and warriors, rather than productive workers. The nation-state allows for some to experience a degree of normalcy within the powers of the state. The expansionist tendencies of nation-states leads to the development of empire, and in the biblical story, empire is subject to God's judgment. They rise and fall.

[15] *you may indeed set over you a king whom the LORD your God will choose. One of your own community you may set as king over you; you are not permitted to put a foreigner over you, who is not of your own community.* [16] *Even so, he must not acquire many horses for himself, or return the people to Egypt in order to acquire more horses, since the LORD has said to you, "You must never return that way again."* [17] *And he must not acquire many wives for himself, or else his heart will turn away; also silver and gold he must not acquire in great quantity for himself.* [18] *When he has taken the throne of his kingdom, he shall have a copy of this law written for him in the presence of the levitical priests.* [19] *It shall remain with him and he shall read in it all the days of his life, so that he may learn to fear*

> *the LORD his God, diligently observing all the words of this law and these statutes,* ²⁰ *neither exalting himself above other members of the community nor turning aside from the commandment, either to the right or to the left, so that he and his descendants may reign long over his kingdom in Israel.*
>
> DEUT 17:15–20

If Israel today were to follow her Scriptures, then she would enter Gaza with good intent, she would dig wells to provide for the inhabitants of the land. She would, through peaceful processes, dismantle the ideologies of war and the gods of war. In a few generations, Israelis and Palestinians would become a people with an invisible border.

If the church did not idolize all that is Jewish, honoring Israel solely for the sake of blessing without testifying to Israel's need to return to her God, then the church would become a witness for peace, for the Lord of Israel—the Lord of the whole earth.

Reading Thirty-Five

A Cognitive Field of Hermeneutics

The Arrival

Meeting a text
A foreigner, an alien, an exile, a welcome intruder
To read a story is to turn and tell a story
The Master Storyteller who subverts reality with mercy and grace
An interpreter of the text

A Cognitive Field of Hermeneutics

Church tradition in the arena of biblical studies and theology is only a part of the interpretive effort. Interpretation from a cognitive field of hermeneutics, coupled with real-world experience and drawn from the biblical text, is not determined by the claims of church tradition. If this were not so, we would have no need for the continued study of the Scriptures to reveal truth beyond what has already been received. Equating church tradition with the authority of Scripture has historically led to tyranny and brutality. This occurs because church authorities take on the position of absolute knowing and the Spirit is co-opted as subservient to the institution, rather than the teacher of the Way.

The Reformation motto of *Sola Scriptura* is an oxymoron because the reader always brings their person to the text. Scripture in effect is only as good as the person reading it. God-talk is always worked out in the struggle of voices seeking to establish and bring meaning that is true and applicable to life. We can never escape the struggle, but we can advance meaning through good teaching built upon good readings.

A Cognitive Field of Hermeneutics

In this piece I will establish a fluid and open description on my statement, "A Cognitive Field of Interpretation." My intent is to be less than conventional in this presentation of hermeneutical methods, both explored and unexplored. I do not intend to be comprehensive in every area, and I acknowledge each area contains an abundance of subcategories that are individually important, even though they may be basic pedagogue to a person well versed in literature, writing, and interpretive methods. When presenting a category for interpretation that is the product of my own exercise, and I am not aware of other writing on said category, I will present the category as my own inventiveness.

The necessity of a cognitive field of hermeneutics is to avoid the tendency to turn the interpretation of Scripture into a mystic exercise where a person can make Scripture mean anything. Such interpretation abolishes the meaning of Scripture as a medium for assuring theological claims are cognitively verifiable. As a normative guide for basic hermeneutical practice, I will freely function within the Wesleyan Quadrilateral: Scripture, tradition, reason, and experience.

I am tempted to produce a graph with categories and subcategories, but that would not be much fun. Besides, there are lots of books written on hermeneutics, even hermeneutic dictionaries. So, I will provide a cognitive field of hermeneutics through some interpretive readings. The initial task of any interpreter is to read the text itself. Now we may begin.

Every author writes with an intent. Establishing authorial intent is dependent upon other hermeneutical concerns, such as the life setting of both writer and text. I think it is good practice to identify authorial intent, while acknowledging that the intent of the writer is not always determinate for limiting meaning derived from a text. This is so based upon sociological phenomena that can be reflected in a text without the writer's awareness. This means that a writer is located in a certain sociocultural milieu and so this location (setting) contributes to the writer's effort in accepted language and behaviors. Also, claiming divine inspiration and canonical authority can expand the limited intention of the author and place the text as part of a greater whole that can challenge, affirm, or rework the author's intended meaning. For example, it is evident that most (if not all) of the authors of the Psalms did not intend their Psalms to develop a subsequent history of use that expanded their meaning for theological purposes not yet imagined (as was done by the writers of the New Testament).

Everyday Thoughts

The writer of Ecclesiastes (Qohelet) reveals an interesting hermeneutic that is acknowledged when we recognize that Qohelet was written purposefully in a manner that psychologically impacts the reader's senses, emotions, and intellect. In order to uncover this writing practice and interpret the authorial intent of Qohelet it would be helpful to invent a descriptive term or phrase. Perhaps "subversive psychology" would be fitting as a phrase for identifying Qohelet's writing style within the wisdom genre. I would prefer "reader response," but the phrase is taken and does not carry the meaning I'm seeking to identify.

I will explain and use the writing of Qohelet to demonstrate. First, thematic progression within the construct of a biblical book (Job) is already identified as a writing technique that aids the reader in learning. Qohelet uses thematic progression with subtle but important changes to his proverb:

> [15] What is crooked cannot be made straight, and what is lacking cannot be counted.
>
> ECCL 1:15

This proverb establishes part of Qohelet's observation and complaint about reality, about temporality. He alters the proverb later in his writing and provides the reader with the tools to foil the claim made in the proverb's first manifestation.

> [13] Consider the work of God; who can make straight what he has made crooked?
>
> ECCL 7:13

The question answers itself, for only God can correct the immeasurable lack in the temporal world with God's lasting self. The world is lacking God and God is responsible for making a world that is crooked, that is without meaning. Without God there is no meaning. This is the claim of Qohelet.

Now that I have demonstrated part of Qohelet's writing style through thematic progression, I will move on to demonstrate how Qohelet uses subversive psychology to push his reader beyond the limits of physical reality and into grasping transcendence.

Although the genre of Qohelet's book is classified as "wisdom," Qohelet utilizes literary devices common to structuralism. For instance, he bookends his Solomonic personification with a poem. Both poems leave the reader with a silent message: the first poem claims all is temporal (Eccl 1:1–11), and the second acknowledges that life is filled with moments common to all human beings (Eccl 3:1–11). Between these driving forces of poetic impact, the writer has mocked the tradition of Solomon as a practitioner of wisdom and exposed him to have been overcome by the trappings of power and excess. Solomon had not grasped the meaning of life, which is Qohelet's pursuit.

According to Qohelet, all meaning is lost because of the nature of temporality and the finality of death. However, there is a driving force in humanity that objects to the finality of death. Where does this come from?

> [11] *He has made everything beautiful in its time. Also He has put eternity in their hearts, except that no one can find out the work that God does from beginning to end.*
>
> Eccl 3:11

Qohelet points to a discrepancy in creation: humanity has not been created to accept death as a natural end for human life. In the hearts of human beings, God has placed the concept of eternity—of life without end. So, Qohelet digs at this established evidence for God implanted in the very heart of humanity. In a manner, Qohelet has identified a part of what it means to be created in the image of God. Qohelet strikes out at this reality to anger his reader.

> [18] *I said in my heart with regard to human beings that God is testing them to show that they are but animals.* [19] *For the fate of humans and the fate of animals is the same; as one dies, so dies the other. They all have the same breath, and humans have no advantage over the animals; for all is vanity.* [20] *All go to one place; all are from the dust, and all turn to dust again.* [21] *Who knows whether the human spirit goes upward and the spirit of animals goes downward to the earth?*
>
> Eccl 3:18–21

He is relentless in his attack upon meaning and assigns meaninglessness to all that goes on under the sun. Jacques Ellul contends that only the word is not placed under the banner of meaninglessness (*hebel*). This must be so, for the very word that Qohelet writes in order to move his reader towards meaning (chapter 12) ends with judgment. How can judgment be accomplished without the presence of those being judged? To live before God as one to be judged gives meaning to life.

This literary tactic, subversive psychology, forces the reader to reject the claims of meaninglessness bolstered by Qohelet's purposeful rhetoric. Qohelet knows this or he would not have written 3:11.

Qohelet writes in such a way as to change his reader without the reader's awareness of the process. The writer uses devices of structuralism, thematic progression, and provocative speech to incite anger and resolution that ends with a yet-to-be-realized possibility: resurrection. This alone can provide meaning; this can only be accomplished by God. Qohelet, the wise teacher, has exceeded the wisdom of Solomon and found a reason for living that rests in God. Qohelet, the preacher of joy, has turned despair into hope. Who we are and how we live is meaningful, because God cares.

Reading Thirty-Six

The Teacher and Christian Education

Such Wonder
Born with a beginning
Sensations ignite the mind
A mind meeting the world
From dependency to maturity the soul is formed
A child of humanity
A treasure of possibility
Born with the right to inherit, and be taught, the learning of those who are past

Educating for Character

A Christian education is initially rooted in study of the Hebrew and Christian Scriptures. It is the belief that the Scripture addresses the ethical and moral guidelines for every aspect of human life. This belief makes Scripture a relevant source for educational study beyond religious confessions and corporate worship.

Biblical literacy is an imperative for a Christian education. Biblical literacy is the ability of the beneficiary of a Christian education to be able to use the entire corpus of Scripture as a resource for responding to all of life. This means the student's intellectually formed ethic is born of intense study of the Scriptures. In this effort, the ethical teaching of the Rabbis is a beginning model. In light of the gospel and the ongoing study of Christian theology, biblical literacy overcomes the alleged disjunction between the two testaments with a conjunctive theological effort based upon the revelation of God in Jesus' cross and resurrection.

Christian education's guiding principle is the spiritual and ethical formation of the student's character (conformation to the image of God in Christ). This single factor makes Christian education different from the current educational paradigm of awarding student progress based upon test scores. The importance of biblical education precedes the entrance of young people into the world as active participants in the formation of society. Further, it requires that biblical education be valued by the Christian community with the understanding that it embraces all of life's disciplines at an ethical and spiritual level. For example, ideas and content are more important than minor grammatical errors in a student paper. Grammatical errors are easily addressed, ideas and content are superior.

As an intellectual exercise the goal of Christian education is the instruction of students in a manner that enables them to think critically, yet constructively with faith. The study of the Bible must engage the current theories of academic studies of Scripture with openness.

When navigating terrain that violates basic creedal confessions, the student recognizes the error of method but is unafraid to explore contrary ideologies because his/her own faith is firm. The awakening of the human mind is a work of the Spirit, and so a Christian education must appeal to the gifts, talents, and interests of individual students. In doing so, the teacher functions as a mentor. This requires that classes be of a manageable size that maintains personal interaction on a regular basis with the student and the teacher.

As basic pedagogue, Christian educational methods must promote open inquisitiveness in the student that is applicable to every aspect of life. For accomplishing the task of biblical literacy, every book of the Bible must be read line by line with a teacher capable of inspiring student interests through the manner in which the teacher brings the text to life, not simply homiletically but

> As an intellectual exercise the goal of Christian education is the instruction of students in a manner that enables them to think critically, yet constructively with faith.

especially intellectually. The teacher's ability to apply the lessons of the text in multiple ways via the tools of biblical interpretation is an integral part of any successful pedagogue for teaching Scripture. The interpretive tools include insights into the text's structure, the author's intent, the applicable elements of the text into everyday life and associative connections with the larger stream of canonical readings.

Interpretation of Scripture is a theological exercise that applies knowledge to life's affairs. This being said, an education designed for gaining biblical literacy, exposes students to the subjects that form an educated person, meaning the study of Scripture requires exposure to ancient man, anthropology, literary analysis, poetry, narrative philosophy, ecology, the right to build, law, psychology, history, science, math, economics, culture, sociopolitical and global realities, music, medicine, ethics, contemplation on meaning, and humanitarian work, among others.

The dogmatic element of Christian education is limited to those guidelines that define the essential confessional beliefs, which qualify an individual or group as Christian. While there is great diversity in Christian thought, there are qualifying aspects of belief that affirm inclusion into the church. In this respect the creeds serve the church better than denominational statements. Christian education cannot be limited by denominational particulars that are not required for qualifying a person as a believer. Christian education requires freedom for people to think and grow without being judged as an outsider based upon their acceptance or rejection of nonessentials.

The essential aspect of Christian education is the teacher. In Christian education, teaching is more than a profession, it is a calling. The teacher is a minister of learning. The teacher's personality is formed around an intense inquisitiveness about life and the world. The Christian teacher views all of life through a theologically mature lens. In Christian education the teacher must be an exemplar of the faith and not merely a communicator. The teacher must demonstrate an ability to speak intelligently about multiple disciplines without being an expert.

A Christian education is responsible for the passionate humanity, intellectual tenacity, spiritual grounding, and inspiration that forms young people and enables them to excel in their chosen fields of work, life, and study while living an exemplary life of faith.

Reading Thirty-Seven

God of Freedom not of Control

The Living One

Alive
Forming possibility and adventure
Walking among us with the freedom of one no one can bind
Always more than
All the finer traits of humanity springing from the one introducing creation to the living one
Transcendence arrested by omnipotence
God has become free

Free to Choose, to Create Reality

People seem oddly averse to the nature of reality; they prefer to speak of God as having total control and responsibility for every facet of their lives and do not consider that God has relinquished his control over to our freedom of choice. God has also set the cycles of nature that define the limits of human life and understanding. He does not often disrupt the order he has placed in creation, even the unpredictable facets of nature's whims.

> [11] *Again I saw that under the sun the race is not to the swift, nor the battle to the strong, nor bread to the wise, nor riches to the intelligent, nor favor to the skillful; but time and chance happen to them all.*
>
> ECCL 9:11

This theological weakness (belief in fate) produces religious claims that make God complicit for sin and its repercussions in human life. This basic failure allows a person to accept all of reality as God's will. Of course, any believer at this point should be thinking of the Lord's Prayer and recall that Jesus instructed us to pray for the will of God to be done on earth as in the heavenly realm. Simply said, we pray for God's will to be done because it is *not* always done.

It is arguably true that God knew human beings would inevitably fail and pollute reality with sin. A redeeming God cannot be a redeemer without image-bearing creatures to redeem. So, God was willing to allow the suffering caused by the entrance of sin, in order to redeem and reveal God's self through the progressive unfolding of salvation in history. Human beings, bearing the image of God, are interconnected, and each generation leaves an imprint upon the following generation. Further, our technological, legal, sociocultural development, and ideologies are passed along through history from generation to generation.

> Simply said, we pray for God's will to be done because it is not.

[20] *for the creation was subjected to futility, not of its own will but by the will of the one who subjected it, in hope.*

ROM 8:20

I think people would like to believe that meaning is never lost to sin and chance, that absurdity has value, that God is intimately involved in every moment of their life. This utopian hope for God's presence to permeate all of reality is, if you will, a primal need. It is a primal need that is established once the concept of monotheism and a God of love are adopted. As I have stated in other places, the perennial task of theology is to wrestle with how to understand, or reconcile, a just God with an unjust existence.

[24] *The earth is given into the hand of the wicked; he covers the eyes of its judges—if it is not he, who then is it?*

JOB 9:24

The ease with which some people accept all of reality as God's doing is slightly understandable when we look to God as omnific and recognize our finitude. Yet, God's culpability for creation is not absolute in the sense that God shares with humanity the power to create our ideological and relational reality. This means our choices make a difference in the world. Whether good or bad, our choices affect all our relationships and us. Jeremiah will portray God as being surprised by the human propensity to sin.

> ⁷ And I thought, "After she has done all this she will return to me"; but she did not return, and her false sister Judah saw it.
>
> JER 3:7

In the Christian faith, God's culpability is displayed in his redemptive revelation of self through the history of Abraham and his descendants and culminating in his death upon a cross. God's only guilt is that he was merciful enough to choose to create finite beings in his image, knowing that they would fail and need to be redeemed.

> ³⁴ Then Jesus said, "Father, forgive them; for they do not know what they are doing.
>
> LUKE 23:34

Not everything happens for a reason; rather, for those that love him, God causes all things to work together for good and provides a reason where none existed.

> ²⁸ We know that all things work together for good for those who love God, who are called according to his purpose.
>
> ROM 8:28

In the aforementioned verse it is imperative we understand "all things" to include both chance and human choice. "All things" includes the mess we make of our world and our lives. This is good news; it indicates the redemptive practice of God's work in our lives. God can turn a mess into an ordered plan, a tragedy into faith, hardship into character; he walks with us through the valley of death's shadow.

I think it is correct to understand that when the Scripture states that "we" are predestined, it is important to know that our predestination is God's plan of redemption working in our lives to conform us to the image of his Son. Further, the foreknown are the ones that say yes to God. God expects that his active work in the drama of history will not be in vain, but that some will say yes. These make up the collective body referred to as "those whom he foreknew."

> [29] *For those whom he foreknew he also predestined to be conformed to the image of his Son, in order that he might be the firstborn within a large family.*
>
> Rom 8:29

I do not want to solely individualize God's redemptive work in our midst. The individual must recognize the work of God in the history that preceded and produced their life. To excise one's self from the influences of family is to deny the work of God and attempt to excise one's self from history. In order to know one's self, a person must accept their historical existence, both past and present. For many of us, our faith is a product of our family and their history.

The generational reaction to faith development within an historical context is often cyclical. For instance, a generation responds to the present with practices that challenge the world in which they live. The next generation sees their practices in need of some fine-tuning and rejects or improves them for a new liberty. The following generation responds to the new liberty of their parents with some restraint that results in a move towards the practices of the generation of their grandparents. I don't mean to sound hopeless; there is always the exception. And this is the goal, the exceptional life that models Jesus to the world with all the trappings of the present age. A community of exceptional persons is God's mustard seed present in the world.

Our religious practices should not be reactionary, but theologically driven efforts to participate in the redemptive activity of God in the present. We will not correctly identify God's redemptive efforts that work across the generations and work beyond our individual interests if we do not understand the conflict between God and creation.

Creation for God is a great adventure, because God created a world of beings capable of determining their own existence and who require God's revelation and active redemptive efforts in history. Cooperating with God's redemptive work in history requires that we be able to identify how God is working to move us towards the reign of God. We are not actors on a stage; we are full-on improvisational entities making history. We can make

Everyday Thoughts

history with God or against God, and it is imperative that we understand our freedom and not adapt a theology of history as already written.

I want to conclude this article with some ways to cooperate with God in his redemptive work. First, God is merciful (Exod 34:6) and acts of mercy are in harmony with God. If you want to find God in the world, look for mercy. If you want God to join you in your efforts to serve, be merciful. Next, recognize God's heart for the oppressed and seek justice in the world; that is, maintain a preferential option for the poor in all your doings. Also, do not participate in, or justify, violence but seek peace with all your soul. And finally, remember to walk humbly with God; you are not responsible to save the world but to exemplify the Spirit of Christ within the confines of the life God gives you.

> If you want to find God in the world, look for mercy.

Reading Thirty-Eight

Sensitivity to Evil

Where is the seat of evil?
With my eyes open I have found the lair of evil
Navigating human history
A lifeless parasite tearing at the womb of humanity
Human beings cannot rule over one another they are incapable
There is one

Wisdom's Pain

The personification of evil is an inherently problematic practice, because people will seek to inhabit the entirety of evil in another group or person, without recognizing their own participation in the evil that exists in their person or culture or government. This form of self-righteousness lacks the basics of Christian practice: repentance, love for the other, and a healthy understanding on the human condition. Nor is the denial of evil as a power that can concentrate in a group, culture or society a wise practice. The spiritual person should have a discerning sense of evil built upon knowledge of history, theology, and experience.

In recent times, the holocaust is a constant reminder kept before our memories through the efforts of those that understand the power of remembering (history). When the technological advances of the industrial era were put to use with the efficiency of an assembly line system for the extermination of an entire people group, our concepts of progress were annulled. Progress had been summoned to participate in the evil of humanity in an unimaginable way. By the end of this period, humanity's propensity for harnessing power to kill masses of human beings would become even more efficient with the building and use of atomic bombs.

The simple word "remember" demonstrates the possibility of human madness to give birth to the sins of the past with the same delusion of greatness and purpose that inhabited those that murdered their way into power. America's failure to remember her sins (genocidal acts against the American Indian, enslaving African Americans, lynching African Americans, the expansion of U.S. interests into Latin America and Southeast Asia, the Ludlow massacre in Colorado, and the bombing of civilian populations) as a nation is a tragic failure; such remembrance requires repentance of every generation. We are all victims of sin prior to becoming perpetrators of sin. This being said, we must be ever diligent to root out all that is contrary to the Spirit of holiness with grace and wisdom.

> We are all victims of sin prior to becoming perpetrators of sin.

If we do not become children of God, we are children of our fathers and will repeat their sins. Forgetting the past, thinking we are better people than those that lived before us, is a mistake that leads to disaster. Collective repentance wards off the evil of self-righteousness. The ideological powers that legitimized evil are rooted deeply in the fabric of thought, society, language, culture, and government. This being said, we are inheritors of sin. A little ash on the forehead might seem like a ridiculous symbol to us liberated post-moderns, but the meaning of the symbol must be articulated with remembrance of national sins throughout our history.

Understanding evil is an imperative for any person concerned with the flourishing of life. Life cannot flourish when evil is intrinsically sown into the systems by which we live and govern. The human propensity for evil seems to give God pause: "have you eaten from the tree?" (Gen 3:11). The "and I thought . . . she would return to me" of Jeremiah 3:7 further highlights this point. Evil is inconsistent with the imagination of God, as indicated by his surprise at the depths of humanity's capacity for evil: "to burn their sons and their daughters in the fire, which I did not command, *nor did it enter into my mind*" (Jer 7:31).

Sensitivity to evil and discerning evil is not easy in a world of complex social relationships; the writer of Hebrews agrees.

> [12] *For though by this time you ought to be teachers, you need someone to teach you again the basic elements of the oracles of God. You need milk, not solid food;* [13] *for everyone who lives on milk, being still an infant, is unskilled in the word of righteousness.* [14] *But solid*

> *food is for the mature, for those whose faculties have been trained by practice to distinguish good from evil.*
>
> HEB 5:12–14

Sensitivity to evil should be born out of regular experience of the holy, an understanding of the good, and a constant pursuit of the truth. Or, as Heschel proposed was the state of all prophets, an ability to hold God and man in one thought, at one and at all times. Moses once said that he wished all God's people would be prophets. Moses is relating prophesying and receiving the Spirit as equatable with being a prophet. If we can learn to be like a prophet and be a person that speaks with God and humanity held in a single thought, then we will be in a good place.

> Sensitivity to evil is born out of being close to God.

Only God, love, and a real sense of being can enable a person to hold humanity and God in a single thought. To add the rest of Heschel's saying, "at one and at all times" is descriptive of the person that has been appointed of God to speak. Such persons are consumed, their consciousness invaded with the presence of God, speaking for God is their business, they can do nothing else. Sensitivity to evil is born out of being close to God.

Reading Thirty-Nine

God in the Court of Human Experience

Come now O High and Lofty One
I will speak of justice and life under your sun
I will hold you culpable for what you have done
I will even charge you if you will not silence me with your power
All I have left is my cry for a world where justice is done
Out of the goodness you have given me I will challenge your right to judge
My fall was not sin but your pleasure
Testing me to see if I am more than dust and ashes
Hear then the voice of a soul that cannot hide
Sit with me for awhile in your world
Sit beside me as an equal
Now I await for you O lowly man to speak for me

Charging God for the Human Condition

The Hebrew quest for wisdom, for discerning the voice of God through the created order (that is the underlying structures of reality), explores the revelation of God in creation, and seems to neglect the revelation of God in Jewish history. Wisdom in the Bible is a form of "natural theology" and avoids the difficulties of theology drawn from interpreting complex narratives. The wisdom books of Sirach, Wisdom of Solomon, Ecclesiastes, and portions of Proverbs and Psalms reflect Israel's efforts at philosophical theology. Although the book of Job is regularly classified as wisdom literature, it is more a collage of literary art, utilizing multiple genres and a polyphonic method. The intertextual makeup of Job offers Israel a new story outside their history, and offers new theological insights through Job as narrative and as prophetic literature.

The answer to the problem of evil is pursued in the book of Job and the concept of a just God is set against the reality of human experience. The Joban dialogues are an exercise in theodicy, the work of a poetic playwright. The theological genius and inspiration of the writer of Job pushes the envelope of revelation, obtainable through wisdom with fearless honesty. Job refuses to exonerate God for the pain and suffering that he endures. Job's monotheism is radical and has no room for the shifting of blame: God is culpable, and God is the almighty. Job's God is not yet a clear vision of the Abba revealed in Jesus.

Job seeks to bring God into the courtroom of human understanding to face the perceived evil of God's manner for governing existence. With relentless integrity, Job speaks as humanity's representative, voicing the torturous experiences of his life as injustices wrought upon him at the hand of God . . . and he is correct.

There is a conflict in the book of Job: the acceptance of death's permeating presence in creation and the underlying structures of reality are not recognized as a just action. The writer of Job challenges God's claim that we are not fit to live (death), and he does so with a blameless character whose voice can speak freely, without a guilty conscience.

The underlying claim of the author of Job is that the severity of death's sentence is incomprehensible to human beings. Death's voice seeks to claim finality. The image of God in humanity conflicts with death: can that which is eternal (Godlike) die? Our sentience about the image of God in us is an underlying structure of our being. Human sentience knows that killing human beings should not be done; even by God. If death is not received as a just judgment, then human beings justify concepts like survival of the fittest and live accordingly. So Job claims God lacks the experience of human beings and therefore is unfit to judge humanity.

> Our sentience about the image of God in us is an underlying structure of our being.

There is a legitimate complaint on the part of human beings. As mortals born to die, our failures are ensured because we are born to die. From the human perspective, the judgment of death inhibits our ability to do good, and this is true. From God's perspective, the judgment speaks for God on the incompatibility of humanity with God's being. God would have to give of God's self in an intimate, ontologically personal way, which would test his desire for relationship with humanity—the apex of his creative effort.

Only a relational story lived out in struggle seems able to communicate the cost of God's love. God's desire for humanity to know what it means to be holy and to live as holy creatures cannot simply be a state of being at the point of creation. The experiential aspect of reality is essential to the process of knowing. So Job responds:

> [4] *Do you have eyes of flesh? Do you see as humans see?* [5] *Are your days like the days of mortals, or your years like human years?*
>
> JOB 10:4–5

This piece of the dialogue seeks to validate human experience as essential for God to possess if God is to be just in his judgments. The mythopoeic story of The Fall is now set in contrast to the mythopoeic blameless man, born east of Eden. The creature cries out to his Creator and will not relent as long as he is not overcome by the fearful grandeur of God's being.

The dialogues of Job with his friends and his God come to a close. Job's questions are left unanswered. Job lives on the side of revelation history that precedes the coming of God in Christ Jesus. Yet, the incarnation of God in flesh answers Job's claim. God must become a human being if he is to fully grasp the reality of human existence. Has Job in one sense won a victory, or has Job recognized a great theological reality? Has Job's driving honesty brought him closer to truth? I think so; however, the theological dialogues must continue as the revelation of God progresses towards resurrection.

The ending of Job is unsatisfactory; his suffering was real and has touched him deeply. The pain and loss of the lives of his children is not undone by the birth of more children. God did not appear before Job as a friend or a father figure. God appeared to Job in power, seeking to be understood but unable to communicate God's self. Job was silenced by the fear and dread of a creator that brings death and life.

The creature created in the image of God, inheritor of a moral conscience, appeals to God with the morality and the intellect given to him by his Creator, and his voice is granted legitimacy because God affirms his speech and ultimately becomes a human being.

From God's perspective, his judgment of death upon humanity is just and essential. Yet, he is God and not a man (until Christ), and he will meet the creation in a manner that serves God's desire for humanity to know him. The drama of human existence is inexorably linked to the drama of God's desire to be known through the process of revelation played out on the stage of history.

The biblical quest for wisdom is an ongoing activity. The wisdom books are models for honesty when thinking about God and world. The ongoing dialogue and pursuit to understand God's work in creation must press forward beyond the strictures of Job. The revelation of God in Christ must be applied to the questions that rise up in us.

Reading Forty

Reading the Lazarus Stories

Where Are the Children of Lazarus?

*The Children of Lazarus
Laid at the gate of our lives
Displayed like pictures without a frame
Crumbs of refuse is their livelihood
Tokens of help is the only bread we provide
With a conscience relieved we go about our lives
Lazarus' invisible children are now in paradise
Hung on the cross of progress*

God Helps

The two Lazarus stories are found in the gospels of Luke and John. They, of course, are not synoptic stories but completely different stories with one major commonality: the name Lazarus. However, the name of the main character is not the only connection that the two stories possess. They both present a theological truth that challenges our senses, our reasoning. These two stories teach us there is a witness in the world that is more powerful, more important, than seeing or speaking with a human being raised from the dead—specifically, it is the witness of the Spirit that accompanies the Scripture.

Luke's story of Lazarus and the Rich Man is a fictional theological parable. His initial introduction of the two major characters leaves both nameless and contrasts their socioeconomic divide. They are identified as "poor man" and "rich man." The universal application of the story addresses the responsibility of those with the world's goods to respond to the needs of those persons laid at the gate. When the poor man is named in the parable, it is the meaning of the name that is important for interpreting the story. The name Lazarus is derived from the Hebrew Eleazar, which means, "God helps."

The meaning of the name Lazarus prompts us to look for the help that God provides, because at first, it appears, God does not help Lazarus. However, the teaching of the parable is clear: I am responsible for the one laid at the gate of my life. On the other hand, the rich man's failure to help the poor man resulted in his painful separation from Abraham. In the parable, the only reason the rich man is in Hades is because he refused to help the poor man.

> In the parable of the rich man and Lazarus the only reason the rich man is in Hades is because he refused to help the poor man.

Even from Hades the rich man views Lazarus as someone to do his bidding. Lazarus remains a lesser person in the eyes of the rich man, in spite of his intolerable existence away from the bosom of Abraham. Lazarus will not cross the divide to bring relief to the rich man because the chasm is born of the rich man's own construction. The rich man requests that Lazarus might go and warn his brothers about the end of their manner of living, which justifies wealth and ignores the suffering. The parable closes with the following lines.

> [29] Abraham replied, "They have Moses and the prophets; they should listen to them." [30] He said, "No, father Abraham; but if someone goes to them from the dead, they will repent." [31] He said to him, "If they do not listen to Moses and the prophets, neither will they be convinced even if someone rises from the dead."
>
> LUKE 16:29–31

The last line of this parable makes an important theological claim about proofs, signs, and reports on near-death or even resurrection testimonies. In Luke's story, Jesus places the testimony of the Scriptures above such testimonies. The resurrection addressed is a temporary resurrection, like the son of the widow from Nain, or the Lazarus of John 11. Yet, being an eyewitness to the resurrection of Jesus is not essential for belief.

> [29] Jesus said to him, "Have you believed because you have seen me? Blessed are those who have not seen and yet have come to believe."
>
> JOHN 20:29

Jesus pronounces a blessing on people that come to belief without being eyewitnesses to his resurrection. This statement of Jesus seems to derive from similar thinking contained within the last line of Luke's parable. The writings of Moses and the prophets contain the progressive revelation of God in the context of Israel's history. Resurrection is a sign that attests to the message of truth found in the gospel, and is a matter of faith. Proof is not compatible with faith or possible in relation to believing in God.

The Power that Requires Faith as Response

Prior to continuing on this line of thought, the witness of Scripture is the power that requires faith as a response. We will note one of the connective links of John's Lazarus story with Luke's. John's Lazarus (John 11) is raised from the dead, yet in John's gospel this sign results in the religious powers' attempt to kill Jesus (and Lazarus). The powerful fear the Romans more than they do a man that can raise the dead to life. The resurrection of Lazarus is not as convincing as we think it should be. Another interesting testament to the inability of resurrection to prompt faith's response is part of the Great Commission.

> [17] *When they saw him, they worshiped him; but some doubted.*
>
> MATT 28:17

Since most of us have never witnessed a resurrection, or met a person that died and was resurrected, we think of the event as absolute evidence of God's power. However, the testimony of Scripture does not confirm this thinking and even subjects it to doubt. The problem with the resurrection of Lazarus is that he is still subject to death and can be killed. Simply said, God cannot prove himself to be God; faith is always required.

> The world is not a suitable place for Jesus until the time he returns to transform all of creation.

Jesus' death is followed by his ascension into the heavenly realm, where he is not subject to the presence, causes, and afflictions of death. The world is not a suitable place for Jesus until the time he returns to transform all of creation. However, Jesus is now present through the Spirit, the Spirit of Christ. Jesus' resurrection represents a new humanity, free from the power of death. Yet, it is not essential that we see the resurrected Lord with our eyes, but that we hear the testimony of the Spirit attesting to the truth of the Scripture and believe.

In Luke's parable, it is hearing and obeying the teaching of the Hebrew Scriptures that are presented as a superior witness to the rich man's differentiating practices that relieves him from social responsibility for the poor. The rich man's lineage, his blessing (wealth), and his understanding of religion were insufficient to preserve his peace in the afterlife. The rich man did not love God because he was incapable of recognizing God in his neighbor (Lazarus). The rich man devalued Lazarus and valued the temporal constructs of power that had sheltered him from suffering.

In John's story, a man named Lazarus is loved by Jesus and resurrected. However, John's Lazarus sits in contrast to Luke's. John's Lazarus is the brother of Martha and Mary who knew Jesus and supported his ministry. Martha and Mary are likely a part of the group of women in Luke 8:1–3. Unlike Luke's Lazarus, the Lazarus of John's gospel is not a fictional representation but a living person who knew Jesus. Lazarus of Bethany appears to be a fairly well-to-do male, providing care for his sisters. The tomb and the appearance of socially elite religious leaders at Lazarus' funeral, along with Mary's anointing of Jesus with expensive ointment, suggest a well-to-do family. A poor Lazarus in Luke, a well to do Lazarus in John, and God cares for both of them. One dies but continues to live, comforted in the arms of Israel's father. The other dies but lives to continue aiding Jesus in his mission.

Signs like the resurrection of a human being from the dead are testimonies to God's power. Signs can only draw attention, but the word connects the seeker with the Spirit. It is through contemplation and learning of the word of God that the Spirit speaks to us. Learning, knowing, and articulating the gospel are the product of listening to God. Signs do not speak, they only gain our attention, they produce awareness of some reality, but God speaks.

Those persons resurrected by Jesus do not speak; their testimonies are concealed from us. The blood of innocent victims like Abel cries out to God. If we have hearts like God, we will hear their cries. If we study the Scripture, we will find fellowship in the Spirit with God and our fellow human beings.

www.ingramcontent.com/pod-product-compliance
Lightning Source LLC
Chambersburg PA
CBHW071427160426
43195CB00013B/1833